The Complete Guide to DIY

GREENHOUSES

Updated 2nd Edition

Build Your Own Greenhouses, Hoophouses, Cold Frames & Greenhouse Accessories

COOL
SPRINGS
PRESS
Home and Garden Experts

MINNEAPOLIS, MINNESOTA

Quarto is the authority on a wide range of topics.

Quarto educates, entertains and enriches the lives of our readers—enthusiasts and lovers of hands-on living.

www.quartoknows.com

© 2017 Quarto Publishing Group USA Inc.

First edition published in 2011 as *The Complete Guide to Greenhouses and Garden Projects* by Creative Publishing international. This edition published 2017 by Cool Springs Press, an imprint of Quarto Publishing Group USA Inc., 400 First Avenue North, Suite 400, Minneapolis, MN 55401 USA. Telephone: (612) 344-8100 Fax: (612) 344-8692

quartoknows.com
Visit our blogs at quartoknows.com

Cool Springs Press titles are also available at discounts in bulk quantity for industrial or sales-promotional use. For details contact the Special Sales Manager at Quarto Publishing Group USA Inc., 400 First Avenue North, Suite 400, Minneapolis, MN 55401 USA.

10 9 8 7 6 5 4 3 2 1

ISBN: 978-1-59186-674-9

Library of Congress Control Number: 2016962897

Acquiring Editor: Mark Johanson
Project Manager: Madeleine Vasaly
Art Director: Brad Springer
Layout: Danielle Smith-Boldt

Printed in China

NOTICE TO READERS

For safety, use caution, care, and good judgment when following the procedures described in this book. The publisher and BLACK+DECKER cannot assume responsibility for any damage to property or injury to persons as a result of misuse of the information provided.

The techniques shown in this book are general techniques for various applications. In some instances, additional techniques not shown in this book may be required. Always follow manufacturers' instructions included with products, since deviating from the directions may void warranties. The projects in this book vary widely as to skill levels required: some may not be appropriate for all do-it-yourselfers, and some may require professional help.

Consult your local building department for information on building permits, codes, and other laws as they apply to your project.

Contents

The Complete Guide to
DIY Greenhouses

Introduction

A greenhouse may seem like a luxury, because that's exactly what it is—an everyday luxury. It is an extraordinary structure that can, if used correctly, pay for itself. A greenhouse allows you to grow exactly the ornamentals and edibles you want, rather than settling for those that you find in local nurseries and home centers. More than that, the right greenhouse in the right location is a gardener's getaway, a tiny slice of tropical paradise that makes bitter winter cold disappear (if only for an hour or so) and provides a lush vacation spot steps from your back door.

Small home "hobby" greenhouses for the masses are a relatively recent historical phenomenon; the evolution of the greenhouse is grounded in the whims of the wealthy. The first recorded use of hotbeds and cold frames was ensuring Roman emperors had cucumbers in winter. The English greenhouse culture that is so pervasive in the United Kingdom today began on the estates of the landed gentry—aristocrats who wanted fresh citrus and pineapples without the bother of importing those delicacies.

Ultimately, however, the idea of growing crops out of season or out of locality was far too appealing to be confined to the rich. Home gardeners of more modest means soon adopted simpler greenhouses so that they could have fresh vegetables all year round, or get a jump on flowers for their gardens, and that promise is still what draws home gardeners to greenhouses today.

Wonder if a greenhouse would be right for you? Ask yourself a few basic questions: Are you ready to start your own flower-bed showoffs rather than buying flat after flat at the local nursery each spring? Would you like the satisfaction and flavor of growing your own super-healthy greens, fruits, and vegetables? Would you like to experiment with crops that normally would not grow in your zone, including tropical plants like orchids, avocadoes, and pineapples? If the answer to any of these is yes, it's time to consider which greenhouse is best for you.

Before taking the plunge, you'll need to consider the many factors and options that go into setting up a greenhouse. No worries: we've covered all those basics in the pages that follow, leading you to choices based on what you want to grow and how you want to grow it.

Fortunately, a greenhouse need not break the bank. You can find an entire spectrum of prefabricated types, from zip-up plastic covers over hutch-sized metal frames all the way up to house-sized "conservatories" that can dominate a large property. The range of available prefabricated sizes, materials, and technologies ensures that there is a greenhouse for everyone—and if you can't find exactly what you want from a manufacturer, you can build your own. You'll find many wonderful possibilities in the project section of this book.

A greenhouse is even more productive and rewarding when coupled with features such as seed starter racks, custom workbenches, and cost-saving graywater systems. You can also supplement the bounty of the greenhouse with structures such as covered raised beds and portable cold frames that help keep plants warm and protected in garden beds. You'll find a wealth of these "greenhouse complements" in the projects section as well.

Greenhouses

Enter a greenhouse and you've crossed the threshold of an extraordinary place. You're greeted by a profusion of flowers and the rich textures of foliage. Sweet fragrances mix with the earthy smell of soil. Diffused light shines through the misty air. In the silence, you can almost hear the plants growing. Traffic rumbles by unnoticed, and the distractions of the "real" world seem miles away.

Although the experience is similar from greenhouse to greenhouse, the structures themselves are amazingly diverse. They can be large and complex or small and simple. They can be unheated or heated, built of glass or covered in plastic. You'll find greenhouses on city rooftops and tucked into suburban gardens. No two are identical, even if they're constructed from the same kit; the contents of a greenhouse make it unique. Some house vegetables (tomatoes and cucumbers), some shelter tropicals (scheffleras and dieffenbachias), and some are home to flats of germinating begonias. This section is focused on leading you through the many variables among greenhouses. Finding the perfect structure for you and what you want to grow means making the right decisions along the way. The sections that follow will help you do that.

In this chapter:
- Choosing a Greenhouse
- Where to Site Your Greenhouse
- Greenhouse Elements
- Greenhouse Styles
- Gallery of Greenhouses

Choosing a Greenhouse

Greenhouses can take many forms, from simple, three-season A-frame structures to elaborate buildings the size of a small backyard. They can be custom designed or built from a kit, freestanding or attached, framed in metal or wood, glazed with plastic or glass. Spend a little time researching online greenhouse suppliers and you'll discover almost unlimited options. Although it's important to choose a design that appeals to you and complements your house and yard, you'll need to consider many other factors when making a decision. Answering the following questions will help you determine the type, style, and size of greenhouse that suits your needs.

How Will the Greenhouse Be Used?

What do you plan to grow in your greenhouse? Are you mostly interested in extending the growing season—seeding flats of bedding plants early in the spring and protecting them from frost in the fall? Or do you want to grow flowers and tropical plants year-round?

Your intentions will determine whether you need a heated greenhouse. Unheated greenhouses, which depend solely on solar heat, are used primarily to advance or extend the growing season of hardy and half-hardy plants and vegetables. Although an unheated greenhouse offers some frost protection, it is useful only during spring, summer, and fall, unless you live in a warm climate.

A heated greenhouse is far more versatile and allows you to grow a greater variety of plants. By installing equipment for heating, ventilation, shading, and watering, you can provide the perfect environment for tender plants that would never survive freezing weather.

THE COST QUESTION

The cost of a basic freestanding greenhouse can range from the very economical (plastic sheeting and PVC hoop frame) to the surprisingly expensive (custom-designed and built). It all depends on your tastes and aspirations, and on your budget. The following real-life samples will give you a sense of the cost variations (remember, though, that prices can vary widely, depending on features and accessories you choose to include):

- A 5 × 5' pop-up mini greenhouse from one mail order source sold for around $125.

- A small, 6 × 8' greenhouse with rigid polycarbonate panels sold for around $400.

- A more spacious 8 × 17' rigid panel kit with motorized windows sold for around $5,000.

- The most elaborate polycarbonate kit greenhouses we found, available by mail order, sold for around $7,500 for an 11 × 24' structure.

- For a custom-designed and built greenhouse of the same size (11 × 24'), one homeowner recently spent $23,000—a price that could have been much higher for a greenhouse designed with ornamental metalwork or stone foundations.

- A 20 × 30' hoop kit using plastic sheeting and PVC tubing was recently available for around $1,500.

How you plan to use the greenhouse will also determine its size, type, and location. If you only want to harden off seedlings or extend the growing season for lettuce plants and geraniums, a small, unheated structure covered with polyvinyl chloride (PVC) sheeting or even a cold frame—a glass- or plastic-topped box on the ground—might be all you need. If your intentions are more serious, consider a larger, more permanent building. A three-season greenhouse can be placed anywhere on your property and might even be dismantled in the winter, whereas year-round use calls for a location near the house, where utilities are convenient and you don't have to trek a long way in inclement weather.

There are many different reasons to choose a given greenhouse. The owner of this yard opted for a traditional crested, aluminum-framed, glass-enclosed model. The use of clear glass instead of semiopaque plastic allows the greenhouse to be used for meals and relaxing (thus, the table) as well as growing favorite plants.

Attached to the exterior wall of the house, this lean-to-style greenhouse has all the features for complete growing success: running water (A); electrical service (B); a heated plant-propagation table (C); a heater (D) for maintaining temperatures on cold nights; ventilating windows (E) and sunshades (F) for reducing temperatures on hot days; drip irrigation system (G) for maintaining potted plants; a full-length potting bench (H) with storage space beneath; paved flooring (I) to retain solar heat.

Do I Want a Lean-to or a Freestanding Greenhouse?

Greenhouse styles are divided into two main groups: attached lean-tos and freestanding. Lean-tos are attached to the house, the garage, or an outbuilding, usually on a south-facing wall. An attached greenhouse has the advantage of gaining heat from the house. It's also conveniently close to plumbing, heating, and electrical services, which are required to operate a heated greenhouse.

Lean-tos come in just as many variations as full-scale freestanding greenhouses do. This means you can find or build a lean-to that suits an end- or side-wall space and the style of your home. As with greenhouses, lean-tos can be simple enclosed structures meant to be used in three seasons or they can include vent fans, misters, heaters, and the other accessories that increase the usefulness of the structure.

On the downside, lean-tos can be restricted by the home's design. They should be built from materials that complement the existing structure, and a low-slung roofline or limited exterior wall space can make them difficult to gracefully incorporate. Siting can be tricky if the only available wall faces an undesirable direction. In cold climates, they must be protected from heavy snow sliding from the house roof. Lean-tos are typically smaller than freestanding greenhouses and can be subject to overheating if they aren't vented properly.

Standalone greenhouses can be portable or permanent. It's wise to keep that in mind if you anticipate moving in the near future or just aren't certain exactly where you want to fit the greenhouse into your existing landscape.

A freestanding greenhouse can be sited anywhere on the property and is not restricted by the home's design. It can be as large or as small as the yard permits. Because all four sides are glazed, it receives maximum exposure to sunlight. However, a freestanding structure is more expensive to build and heat, and depending on its size, it may require a concrete foundation. Utilities must be brought in, and it is not as convenient to access as a lean-to. Because it is more exposed to the elements, it can require sturdier framing and glazing to withstand winds. You can also secure lighter greenhouses with an anchoring system.

HEATED GREENHOUSE ENVIRONMENTS

Heated greenhouses can be classified by three temperature categories: cool, warm, and hot. Each of these environments supports different plants and gardening activities.

Cool Minimum Nighttime Temperature: 45°F (7°C)
In a cool environment, you can start seeds and propagate cuttings early in the year so they will be ready for planting in garden beds at the beginning of summer. Unless your climate is mild, however, you'll probably need a propagator to provide a little extra warmth for starting seeds. Vegetables and hardy and half-hardy plants do well in this type of greenhouse. Although the temperature in a cool greenhouse is suitable for protecting frost-tender plants, their growth during winter is minimal.

Warm Minimum Nighttime Temperature: 55°F (13°C)
A warm greenhouse is suitable for propagating plants, raising seedlings, and growing a wide range of plants, including flowers, fruits, houseplants, and vegetables, even during the coldest months. You can sow tomato seeds in January and harvest the ripe fruits in June. Though this type of greenhouse provides a highly desirable environment for plants, heating it can be extremely costly, especially if you live in an area with long, cold winters.

Hot Minimum Nighttime Temperature: 65°F (18°C)
Only a few serious gardeners will invest in a hot greenhouse because it is prohibitively expensive to heat. This type of environment is ideal for growing exotic tropical plants, such as orchids, bromeliads, and ferns.

How Big Should the Greenhouse Be?

In all likelihood, you'll shop for a greenhouse that fits the "hobby" category. Larger, estate greenhouses are categorized as "conservatories," while much smaller greenhouses, which are usually portable, are labeled "mini."

Some experts recommend buying the largest greenhouse you can afford, but this isn't always the best advice. You don't want to invest in a large greenhouse only to discover that you're not up to the work it involves.

Of course, buying a greenhouse that is too small can lead to frustration if your plant collection outgrows the space. It is also much more difficult to control the temperature. One compromise is to buy a greenhouse that's one size larger than you originally planned, or better yet, to invest in an expandable structure. Many models are available as modules that allow additions as your enthusiasm grows.

When choosing a greenhouse, take into account the size of your property. How much space will the structure consume? Most of the expense comes from operating the greenhouse, especially during winter. The larger the structure, the more expensive it is to heat.

Be sure the greenhouse has enough room for you to work. Allow space for benches, shelves, tools, pots, watering cans, soil, hoses, sinks, and a pathway through the plants. If you want benches on both sides, choose a greenhouse that is at least 8 feet wide by 10 feet long. Give yourself enough headroom, and allow extra height if you are growing tall plants or plan to hang baskets.

How Much Can I Afford to Spend on a Greenhouse?

Your budget will influence the type of structure you choose. A simple hoop greenhouse with a plastic cover is inexpensive and easy to build. If you're handy with tools, you can save money by buying a kit, but if the greenhouse is large, requires a concrete foundation, or is built from scratch, you may need to hire a contractor, which will add to the cost.

Location is important. If you live in a windy area, you'll need a sturdy structure. Buying a cheaply made greenhouse will not save you money if it fails to protect your plants or blows away in a storm. And cutting costs by using inefficient glazing will backfire because you'll wind up paying more for heating.

BUILDING DEPARTMENT QUESTIONS

Local building codes will vary from region to region, but many dictate the type, size, and location of any greenhouse that may be placed on your property. Codes may also require a certain type of glazing—for instance, they may mandate that in a structure with glass panes, only tempered glass be used. That's why it's essential to do a little homework before you commit to buying or building your dream greenhouse. Here are a few basic questions every homeowner should ask his or her local building department before committing to a specific greenhouse:

- What type of foundation is required for a freestanding greenhouse? If compacted gravel is allowed as a foundation, how deep must the foundation go?

- Is there a minimum wind load required? Are anchors required? (Anchors are necessary for lighter greenhouses in areas that are commonly affected by high winds or extreme weather events.)

- What is the snow load per square foot or dead load required on the greenhouse?

- Does the structure need to be code compliant with the International Building Code (IBC) or Universal Building Code (UBC)? Which year?

- Do the building plans have to be site specific?

- Does the greenhouse have to be Americans with Disabilities Act (ADA) compliant?

How Much Time am I Prepared to Invest in a Greenhouse?

You may have big dreams, but do you have the commitment to match? Maintaining a successful greenhouse requires work. It's not hard labor, but your plants depend on you for survival. Although technology offers many time savers, such as automated watering and ventilation systems, there's no point in owning a greenhouse if you don't have time to spend there. Carefully assess your time and energy before you build,

You might save money by choosing a smaller greenhouse, but if you don't have usable room to grow everything you want to grow, you aren't getting real value out of the structure. This beautiful redwood-framed, prefab unit may be a little pricey, but it offers abundant counter, shelf, and work-surface space as well as quality construction and glazing meant to last decades.

Where to Site Your Greenhouse

When the first orangeries were built, heat was thought to be the most important element for successfully growing plants indoors. Most orangeries had solid roofs and walls with large windows. Once designers realized that light was more important than heat for plant growth, they began to build greenhouses from glass.

All plants need at least 6 (and preferably 12) hours of light a day year-round, so when choosing a site for a greenhouse, you need to consider a number of variables. Be sure that it is clear of shadows cast by trees, hedges, fences, your house, and other buildings. Don't forget that the shade cast by obstacles changes throughout the year. Take note of the sun's position at various times of the year: A site that receives full sun in the spring and summer can be shaded by nearby trees when the sun is low in winter. Winter shadows are longer than those cast by the high summer sun, and during winter, sunlight is particularly important for keeping the greenhouse warm. If you are not familiar with the year-round sunlight patterns on your property, you may have to do a little geometry to figure out where shadows will fall. Your latitude will also have a bearing on the amount of sunlight available; greenhouses at northern latitudes receive fewer hours of winter sunlight than those located farther south. You may have to supplement natural light with interior lighting.

To gain the most sun exposure, the greenhouse should be oriented so that its ridge runs east to west (see illustration, below), with the long sides facing north and south. A slightly southwest or southeast exposure is also acceptable, but avoid a northern exposure if you're planning an attached greenhouse; only shade-lovers will grow there.

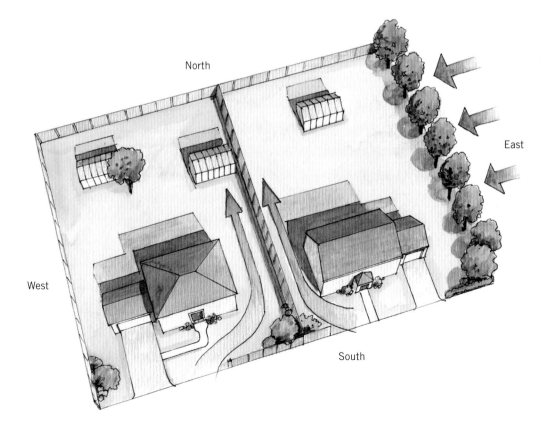

The ideal greenhouse location is well away from trees but protected from prevailing winds, usually by another structure, a fence, or a wall.

North

West

South

East

Siting Factors

Several factors influence the decision of where to build your greenhouse. Some pertain to your property, some to the structure, and some to your tastes.

Climate, Shelter & Soil Stability

Your local climate and geography have an impact on the location of your greenhouse. Choose a site that is sheltered from high winds and far enough away from trees that roots and falling branches are not a threat. (Try to position the greenhouse away from areas in which children play, too.) If you live in a windy area, consider planting a hedge or building a fence to provide a windbreak, but be careful that it doesn't cast shade on the greenhouse. Avoid low-lying areas, which are prone to trapping cold, humid air.

The site should be level and the soil stable, with good drainage. This is especially important if heavy rains are common in your climate. You might need to hire a contractor to grade your site.

Access

Try to locate your greenhouse as close to the house as possible. Connecting to utilities will be easier, and you'll be glad when you're carrying bags of soil and supplies from the car. Furthermore, a shorter walk will make checking on plants less of a chore when the weather turns ugly.

Aesthetics

Although you want to ensure that plants have the perfect growing environment, don't ignore aesthetics. The greenhouse should look good in your yard. Ask yourself whether you want it to be a focal point—to draw the eye and make a statement—or to blend in with the garden. Either way, try to suit the design and the materials to your home. Keep space in mind, too, if you think you might eventually expand the greenhouse.

For maximum heat gain, orient your greenhouse so the roof or wall with the most surface area is as close to perpendicular to the sunrays as it can be.

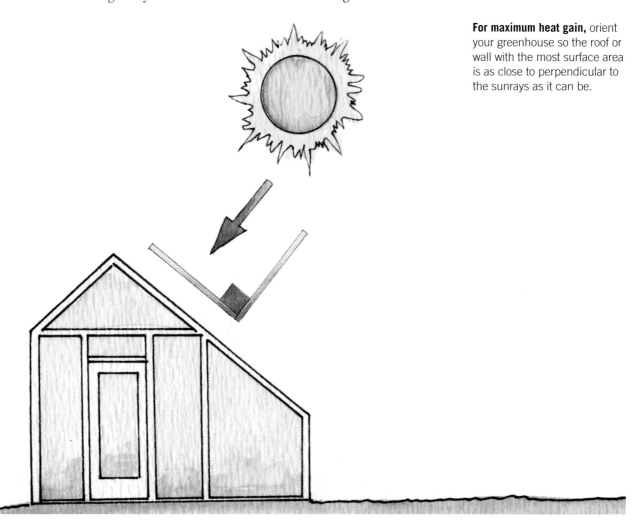

Greenhouse Elements

At first glance, a greenhouse seems like a very simple structure: some basic framing, a good amount of glass or plastic, and voilà—a greenhouse. But actually, there is much more to this garden addition than meets the eye.

In addition to being thoughtfully situated to take advantage of the sun throughout the day and the seasons, any greenhouse must be carefully built to last while still providing an optimal environment for the plants you want to grow. That starts with choosing the right foundation and making sure the greenhouse has an appropriate floor. Not only is the base of a greenhouse important for its support, but the right floor can also serve as a heat sink, absorbing heat during the day and releasing it at night.

In addition, you'll need to put a lot of thought into your greenhouse's covering. Glass is traditional, but fragile and expensive. Plastic panels and sheeting are easier to work with, but you must choose the right type to create the ideal microclimate for your plants.

Any plant needs water, and depending on how large your greenhouse is, you may decide to automate the watering of your plants or to use misters to create the proper humidity. You'll also need to figure out how to moderate the heat inside, because the temperature in a greenhouse can swing by as much as 50 degrees Fahrenheit over the course of any given day. Ventilation goes hand in glove with heat, and, of course, you'll probably want some form of lighting so that you can check on or work with your plants after dark.

These are just some of the factors any greenhouse owner needs to consider and resolve. The purpose of this section is to help you make informed choices from among the great many options available in order to create the ideal space for whatever it is you hope to grow—not to mention yourself.

A greenhouse is composed of several major systems that perform important functions. When planning your greenhouse, you'll need to make choices about each system, which include the foundation, floor, frame, glazing, ventilation, watering, heat, storage, and more.

Foundations

As with a house or any substantial outbuilding, a greenhouse needs an appropriate foundation. For lightweight kits and smaller greenhouses, this may be a compacted gravel base. Larger, heavier structures will most likely require a more significant foundation to prevent movement in the underlying soil from damaging the framing or glazing. A foundation should also keep any wood or metal parts off the ground to prevent premature rot or corrosion.

If you've purchased a kit greenhouse, the manufacturer will likely recommend appropriate foundation options. Regardless of what you're building, you should consult your local building department to determine the codes that dictate the foundation you need to use and whether you need a permit for the foundation, the whole greenhouse, or both.

Whether you're working from codes or simply following best building practices, the foundation needs to match the greenhouse. A kit greenhouse may come with its own metal or fabric base. For many types of prefab structures, a crushed gravel base 4 inches deep or more will serve the purpose.

Other cases may call for a base of landscape timbers, concrete footings or piers, or a concrete slab. More traditional, substantial, and permanent greenhouses are often built on a kneewall of wood, brick, or stone. This is an option for most types of greenhouses, but the work and expense mean that kneewalls are rarely used with hobby greenhouses.

KNEEWALLS

Kneewalls, sometimes called pony walls, are low walls to which a greenhouse frame can be attached. They can raise a greenhouse to maximize headroom and can help to retain heat. However, they also eliminate growing space behind the walls and below the benches. If you only plan to grow potted plants on the benches, this may not be a problem—you can use the area underneath the benches for storage.

Kneewalls can be built with concrete blocks on a concrete footing, but a more attractive option is to use stone or brick and mortar. To help integrate the greenhouse with your home, build the kneewall from materials that complement the exterior of the house.

Earth anchors, or anchor stakes, are often used to tie down very lightweight greenhouses and crop covers to prevent them from blowing away. A typical anchor is a long metal rod with a screw-like auger end that is driven into the ground. An eye at the top end is used for securing a cable or other type of tether attached to the greenhouse.

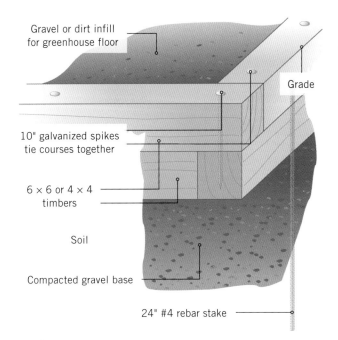

Gravel or dirt infill for greenhouse floor

Grade

10" galvanized spikes tie courses together

6 × 6 or 4 × 4 timbers

Soil

Compacted gravel base

24" #4 rebar stake

Timber foundations are simple frames made with 4 × 4, 6 × 6, or larger landscape timbers. The timber frame is laid over a leveled and compacted gravel base (which can also double as the floor or floor subbase for the greenhouse interior) and pinned to the ground with rebar stakes. One level, or course, of timbers is suitable for small greenhouses, while two courses are recommended for larger structures.

A concrete footing provides a structural base for a large greenhouse or a masonry kneewall. Standard footings are continuous and run along the perimeter of the structure. They must extend below the frost line (the depth to which the ground can freeze in winter; varies by climate) to prevent frost heave and should be at least twice as wide as the greenhouse walls they support.

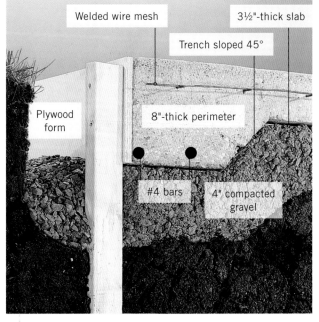

Welded wire mesh

3½"-thick slab

Trench sloped 45°

Plywood form

8"-thick perimeter

#4 bars

4" compacted gravel

Pier footings are structural concrete columns poured in tube forms set below the frost line—the same foundation used to support deck posts. Pier foundations are appropriate for some kit and custom greenhouses and are often used on large commercial hoop-style houses. Anchor bolts embedded in the wet concrete provide fastening points for the greenhouse base or wall members.

Concrete slabs make great foundations and a nice, cleanable floor surface but are overkill for most hobby greenhouses. In some areas, it may be permissible to use a "floating" footing that combines a floor slab with a deep footing edge (shown here). Otherwise, slabs must be poured inside of a perimeter frost footing, as with garage or basement construction. To prevent water from pooling inside the greenhouse, concrete slabs must slope toward a central floor drain—a job for a concrete pro, not to mention a plumber to install the drain and underground piping.

Floors

Even if your greenhouse is small or temporary, a dirt floor is often a bad idea. Watering of plants and even condensation can lead to a muddy mess that invites weeds, disease, and pests. There are plenty of inexpensive options for greenhouse floors, all of which are easy to install yourself. In general, any water-permeable surface that works for a patio or walkway will make a good floor for a greenhouse.

For long-term stability, improved drainage, and a level floor surface, it's wise to support any greenhouse floor with a 4- to 6-inch subbase of compacted gravel. Cover the subbase with commercial-quality landscape fabric (not plastic; the fabric must be water-permeable) to inhibit weed growth and to separate the gravel base

from the upper layers. From there, the simplest floors can be made with any type of suitable gravel, such as pea gravel or trap rock.

Brick and concrete patio pavers are other great options and offer a more finished look and feel over gravel floors. Pavers are laid over a 1- to 2-inch layer of sand and should be surrounded by a border (foundation timbers or patio edging will suffice) to keep them from drifting. Once the pavers are set, you can sweep sand over the surface to fill the cracks and lock the units in place. Another floor option— flagstone—is installed in much the same way. Keep in mind that any stone or concrete surface will also serve as a heat sink. This, alone, can be a good reason to add a stone floor to your greenhouse.

A poured concrete floor is stable and washable, and requires no routine maintenance.

Concrete pavers set in sand offer a longlasting, stable floorcovering that breathes and allows for good drainage.

Pea gravel

Crushed stone

Pathway gravel is the easiest and cheapest flooring to install. Pea gravel, trap rock, and some river stones are good for both drainage and cleanliness. Highly compactible materials, such as decomposed granite, remain solid and level underfoot but leave a lot of grit on your shoes (if that's a concern). In any case, choose a material that's comfortable to walk on; loose or large gravel or stones can be unstable.

Framing Materials

Wood and aluminum remain the most popular framing materials for hobby greenhouses, but they are far from the only options. Steel is popular for larger, more complex structures, and PVC is commonly used for more simple and portable greenhouses and hoophouses.

Every framing option has advantages and disadvantages, which is why it's essential that you choose the best framing material for your needs both now and in the future. The key is to balance durability, weight, expense, and, of course, appearance to find just the right framing. Looking at the tradeoffs entails considering local weather conditions (do you need a high snow or wind load tolerance?), the gardening you intend on doing (do want to hang baskets in the greenhouse?), and the look that most appeals to you (do you want the greenhouse to blend in or stand out?).

A pine frame with plastic glazing. This is a good option for a lightweight and inexpensive greenhouse that will be used for two or three seasons during the year.

Wood

Advantages: Wood is often selected for custom greenhouse framing because of the many beautiful species available. The bonus with a wood frame is that it won't conduct heat as quickly as metal or plastic and will be less likely to shed potentially harmful condensation. It is also long lasting and durable. These qualities come at a higher cost than that of other materials, but the price tag also buys an extremely beautiful greenhouse structure. Some of the best woods for greenhouses are cedar and redwood, because both are naturally resistant to rot and insects and age well, whether finished or unfinished. Hardwoods also offer these benefits, but the cost is usually prohibitive for a hobby greenhouse. The practical choice for a utilitarian greenhouse is pressure-treated wood. In either case, wood is a wise choice if you are planning on hanging baskets or accessories from the framing, or if you intend to put up shelving.

Disadvantages: Wood framing is heavy and usually requires regular maintenance. Because it's necessarily bulkier than other options, wood also casts more of a shadow on greenhouse plants. Rot is a potential problem, especially as the wood ages, and many types of woods will ultimately be attacked by insects—something that is never a problem with plastic or metal. You'll also pay a higher cost for the frame than you would if you had used other materials, especially if you choose the beauty of redwood.

Choose redwood for a greenhouse frame that will last years and provide an incomparable appearance to the structure.

Aluminum

Advantages: The foremost advantage of aluminum is that it is low maintenance. It is also strong and lightweight, lasts longer than wood, and can easily accommodate different glazing systems and connectors. Aluminum is used in many greenhouse kits and can be powder-coated or anodized in various colors (although the most common are white, black, and green). Aluminum greenhouse kits are typically easy to assemble and come with predrilled holes for attachments, connections, and fixtures. Some manufacturers offer "thermally broken" aluminum frames, which are made by sandwiching a thermal barrier between two layers of extruded aluminum to decrease heat loss through the frame.

This simple kit greenhouse includes a basic aluminum frame with durable polycarbonate framing.

An upscale example of a handsome prefab, aluminum-framed greenhouse. The crest and finial are finished in long-lasting baked enamel. A crest like this, as well as adding flair to the greenhouse's look, also keeps birds from perching on the ridge—which in turn keeps the panels cleaner.

Disadvantages: Because aluminum loses heat more rapidly than wood does, this type of greenhouse is more expensive to heat. In addition, cheaper aluminum frames can be too flimsy to withstand high winds or heavy snow loads. The material can also exacerbate condensation problems inside the greenhouse.

Galvanized Steel

Advantages: Galvanized steel frames are most often used for commercial greenhouses because the material is incredibly sturdy, strong, and durable. It can stand up to severe weather and resists corrosion and fatigue.

Disadvantages: This type of framing is some of the heaviest, and framing a hobby greenhouse in galvanized steel will be extremely expensive both to ship and to build. If bumped and scratched, it can be subject to rusting in the scratches, making it better suited to a large structure for which the frame itself won't be buffeted. The protective coating will also wear off with age.

PVC (Polyvinyl Chloride)

Advantages: PVC tubes are used in less expensive kits for hoophouses and greenhouses. The tubes make for a very low-cost frame that is durable and lightweight. The material does not rot and is entirely resistant to insects. It is also easy to clean, and although not distinctive in appearance, it looks neat and tidy. PVC frames are usually used in greenhouses meant to be portable and for beginner or intermediate gardeners.

Disadvantages: High winds, heavy snow loads, and other extreme weather can damage PVC frames. Bright sun also takes its toll, making PVC framing brittle over time. It cannot be used with glass—the frames are restricted to bendable polycarbonate panels or plastic sheeting.

A simple hoophouse frame like this is easy to assemble and doesn't require a serious investment in money or expertise.

Greenhouse Glazing Materials

There are basically two types of greenhouse coverings: glass and plastic. The ideal glazing lets in the maximum amount of light and lets out the minimum amount of heat. But there's more to any greenhouse covering than simply how much sunlight gets through. For instance, if you're growing plants that are sensitive to light overexposure and burning, you may want to opt for an opaque glazing that not only lets less light through but also diffuses the light so that it doesn't concentrate on plant surfaces.

Different materials have different lifespans. Where glass will last as long as the garden does as long as it isn't accidentally broken, polyethylene film is likely to become brittle and fogged after a few years. A good indicator of how long any given material will last is the warranty the manufacturer offers on the panels, sheets, or rolls of the material.

Glass

Advantages: Glass is the traditional material used for greenhouse glazing, and it remains popular today for good reason. If undamaged, the material will last forever. It offers some of the best light transmission among glazing materials, doesn't degrade under long exposure to UV radiation, and is exceedingly easy to clean. It boasts surprising tensile strength—in a frame, it can hold up to a lot of stress and wind load. Although single-pane glazing has poor insulating properties, the R-value can easily be raised by purchasing double- or even triple-pane glazing.

Disadvantages: Uninsulated single-pane glass is very inefficient at retaining heat. Glass is also extremely breakable—children, tree branches, and hail are all threats to a glass greenhouse. For safety, tempered glass is recommended for greenhouses because it shatters when broken, creating small, rounded fragments, rather than sharp, jagged shards. Glass is also heavy, requiring a strong supporting framework that won't flex under stress. Direct sunlight passing through glass is so strong it may burn some plants. Lastly, unlike some synthetic materials and products, glass panes cannot bend to accommodate curved shapes, such as a hoophouse or Gothic arch greenhouse.

Fiberglass

Advantages: Manufacturers have vastly improved fiberglass panel formulation since the material first debuted as a potential substitute for glass panels in homes and outbuildings. Modern fiberglass panels are UV resistant and formulated to resist yellowing under prolonged sun exposure—a key problem in early panels. This material transmits almost as much light as glass does, but also diffuses that light. Fiberglass also provides much better heat retention than glass. The best panels now come with 15- or 20-year warranties.

Disadvantages: The surface of fiberglass panels is rough and captures dirt, requiring more frequent cleanings than other types of glazing. Fiberglass

This stunning redwood greenhouse combines the best of both worlds—the beauty and view through clear glass windows on all walls and frosted polycarbonate panels on the roof to diffuse light.

Fiberglass panels come in clear, white, and colored varieties, such as the green shown here. The ridged panels can be challenging to install, so manufacturers supply wavy nailing strips (called "closure strips") that make installation as easy as nailing flat panels.

panels can also, under certain circumstances, experience excess condensation that can lead to plant disease and overwatering. Dirt and debris can collect in the valleys of panel ridges. Inexpensive fiberglass panels will degrade and deteriorate much more quickly than high-quality versions do.

Acrylic (Plexiglas)

Advantages: Acrylic panels offer excellent light transmission, similar to glass, but in a lighter material that is incredibly durable and impact resistant. The material is also UV resistant and can be molded into unusual shapes. Acrylic is less expensive than polycarbonate, and is easy drill, cut, or shape. It can also be coated to reduce condensation.

Disadvantages: Acrylic has never caught on for use in hobby greenhouses because less-expensive versions have a tendency to yellow with age, and uncoated acrylic is prone to condensation in the temperature extremes of a greenhouse.

Polycarbonate

Advantages: Polycarbonate panels are light, strong, and shatter resistant. Multiwall versions retain heat far better than glass does; the panels are available in basic corrugated form, but the more prevalent types of panels are multiwalled. Manufacturers offer panels with between two and five walls—the more walls, the greater the heat retention and the lower the light transmission. The panels also come in clear and white varieties for greater light diffusion. The material is tough and durable; warranties typically run 10 to 15 years for quality polycarbonate. It is also very easy to work with and difficult to break.

Disadvantages: Although polycarbonate scratches easily, the main drawback to these panels is the high price. They are somewhat hard to clean, because certain mass-market glass cleaners can damage the material.

Polyethylene & PVC

Advantages: Greenhouse sheet coverings—primarily polyethylene plastic, but also including some PVC products—are inexpensive, easy to work with, incredibly lightweight, and adaptable to unusual shapes. They come in different thicknesses, with thicker sheet products slightly better at retaining heat without much loss in light transmission. These products usually come in white (although you can buy clear), which ensures that transmitted light is diffused and won't burn plant leaves. The sheeting can be doubled up, which cuts down significantly on light transmission, or layers can be attached to both the outside and the inside of a structure, for improved heat retention.

Disadvantages: Polyethylene sheeting does not retain heat well and will deteriorate under prolonged sun exposure. The material is prone to rips during installation and can become brittle and yellowed in as little as two years.

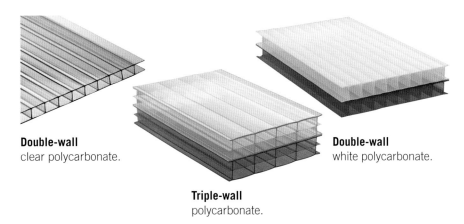

Double-wall
clear polycarbonate.

Triple-wall
polycarbonate.

Double-wall
white polycarbonate.

GREENHOUSE GLAZING CHARACTERISTICS*

GLAZING	LIGHT TRANSMISSION**	R-VALUE	STRUCTURAL STRENGTH
Single-Pane Glass	±95%	.9	High
Double-Pane Glass	±90%	2	High
Double Pane Low E Glass	±70%	3.3	High
Polyethylene Film (6-mil)	±85%	.87	Low
Fiberglass panel	±92%	.9	Medium
Polycarbonate 2-wall (6-mil)	±82%	1.6	Medium
Polycarbonate 3-wall (8-mil)	±76%	2	Medium
Polycarbonate 4-wall (6-mil)	±76%	1.8	Medium
Polycarbonate 5-wall	±62%	3	Medium

*It's important to note that between different manufacturers the same products will vary in light transmission and R-value. The numbers here should be considered for comparison purposes.

**Light transmission will be lower in colored or white panels or film. The variation can be from 90% for clear down to 60% for green in the same material.

Water

All greenhouses need some kind of water supply system. This can be as simple as a hose connected to the nearest outdoor spigot or as complex as a frost-proof underground line extending from your basement to a special hydrant in the greenhouse. The latter is obviously more convenient, and the system can operate year-round. It's also a pretty big job that usually requires a plumber to make the final connections. A somewhat easier alternative is to install a shallow underground water line that you drain at the end of the growing season, similar to the supply line for a sprinkler system. Or, if your water demands are not too great and your greenhouse is located near your house, maintain a rain barrel nearby.

A rain barrel can provide a ready supply of water for your greenhouse. It's an easy water supply option, but it lacks the convenience of linking the greenhouse to your house's water supply system.

 AN ALL-SEASON WATER SUPPLY

A dedicated all-season water line is the ultimate setup for any freestanding greenhouse. To prevent the line from freezing during winter, the entire buried portion of the water line must be laid 6" below the frost line in your area. In the greenhouse, the water comes up through a freeze-proof yard hydrant (commonly used on farms), which drains itself of residual water each time it is shut off. The water drains into a gravel pit (installed per local code and the hydrant manufacturer).

In a typical installation, the supply line connects to a cold-water pipe in the house and includes a shutoff valve and backflow preventer (vacuum breaker). The line passes through the foundation wall (where it's protected by a sleeve of rigid pipe) at the burial depth, then runs underground to the hydrant. For most applications, flexible PE (polyethylene) tubing is the best all-around option for the buried portion of the supply line. As always, all connections and devices must follow local code requirements.

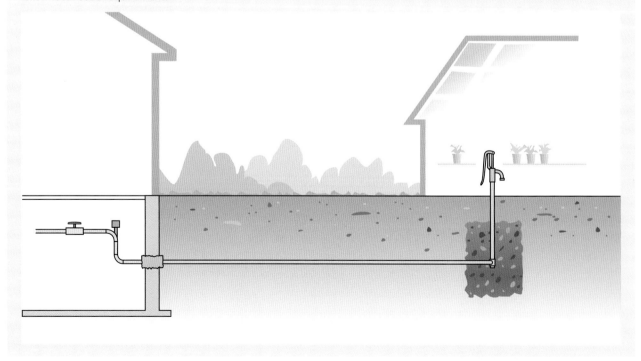

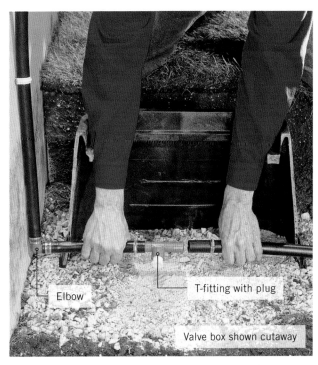

Elbow

T-fitting with plug

Valve box shown cutaway

A seasonal water supply line is similar to an all-season setup but somewhat easier to install and is just as convenient for everyday use. The supply line connects to a cold-water pipe inside the house and runs through an exterior wall above the foundation, then down into a trench (left photo). At the house-end of the trench, the initial supply run connects to the underground line (typically PE tubing) inside a valve box. The box provides easy access to a T-fitting necessary for freeze-proofing the line each fall. The supply run is buried in a 10"-deep trench (or per local code) and connects to copper tubing and a standard garden spigot inside the greenhouse.

Winterize a seasonal supply line using a shutoff valve with an air nipple. With the valve closed and the greenhouse spigot open, blow compressed air (50 psi max.) into the line to remove any water in the tubing. Then, remove the plug from the T-fitting inside the valve box (photo top right) and store it for the winter.

A greenhouse with a water supply of any sort should also have a drain. A dry well can be made with an old trash can or other container perforated with holes and filled with coarse rock. The well sits in a pit about 2' in diameter by about 3' deep and is covered with landscape fabric and soil. Dry wells are for draining graywater only—no animal waste, food scraps, or hazardous materials.

Watering & Misting Systems

If your greenhouse is fairly small and you enjoy tending plants daily—pinching off a spent bloom here, propping up a leaning stem there—you might enjoy watering by hand, either with a watering can (which is laborious, no matter how small the greenhouse) or with a wand attachment on a hose. Hand-watering helps you to pay close attention to plants and cater to their individual needs. You'll quickly notice signs of over- or under-watering and can adjust accordingly.

However, hand-watering isn't always practical. That's why many greenhouse gardeners use an automatic system such as overhead sprinkling and drip irrigation. This approach is convenient, especially when you're not at home. Greenhouse suppliers sell kits as well as individual parts for automated watering systems. Be sure your system includes a timer that can be set to deliver water at specific times of the day, for a set duration, and on specific days of the week. You can also incorporate water heaters and fertilizer injectors into your system.

Overhead-sprinkler systems are attached to the main water supply and use sprinkler nozzles connected to PVC pipes installed above the benches. The system usually includes a water filter, which prevents the nozzles from clogging, and a pressure regulator. Set the system to water in the morning and during the hottest part of the day. Avoid watering late in the day so the plants will be dry before nightfall, when the temperature drops and dampness can cause disease.

Drip-irrigation systems use drip emitters to water plants a drop at a time, when moisture is needed. Each plant has an emitter attached to feeder lines that connect to a drip line of PVC tubing or pipe. Unlike overhead sprinklers, drip irrigation ensures that the plant leaves stay dry. It also helps to conserve water.

If you prefer to water plants from underneath, consider capillary mats. These feltlike mats are placed on top of the bench (which is first lined with plastic) and under the plants, with one end of the mat set into a reservoir attached to the bench. The reservoir

This automatic drip-watering system is fed by a garden hose that connects to the mixing tank. In the tank, water and fertilizer are blended to a custom ratio and then distributed to plants at an adjustable rate via a network of hoses, drip pins, and Y-connectors.

NOTE: The spiral trellis supports hanging from the greenhouse roof are not part of the watering system.

Misting is a very gentle method of providing moisture to plants. Misting heads mounted on spray poles (inset) can be controlled manually or automatically. In addition to maintaining a constant state of moistness for plants, a misting system will give your greenhouse a tropical environment that many gardeners enjoy.

ensures that the mat is constantly moist. Moisture from the mat is drawn up into the soil and to the plant roots when the soil is drying out. Unlike drip irrigation and overhead sprinkling, capillary-mat watering systems do not require electricity, pipes, or tubing. However, unless they are treated, the mats will need regular cleaning to prevent mildew and bacteria buildup. To ensure that the system works properly, it's important that the bench be level.

Regardless of the watering system you choose, use lukewarm water. Cold water can shock the roots, especially if the soil is warm. If you're hand-watering, let the water sit in the greenhouse so it warms up to ambient temperature. (Keep it out of the sun, though—you don't want it to get too hot). Wand watering and automatic systems can benefit from an installed water heater.

Misting

When the temperature inside the greenhouse rises and the vents open, they release humidity. Misting increases humidity, which most plants love—levels of about 50 percent to 65 percent are ideal—and dramatically decreases the temperature by as much as 20 degrees Fahrenheit. Misting systems are available through greenhouse suppliers. You can buy a complete system, which may include nozzles, tubing, PVC pipe, a humidistat, and sometimes a hard-water filter and a pressure gauge. Or you can buy the parts separately to create a customized system. The size of the greenhouse will determine the size of the system. Larger greenhouses need more nozzles and in turn more tubing and pipe.

Humidistats can automatically turn on misters and humidifiers when the humidity drops below a set level. You might also want to invest in a device to boost the water pressure. Higher pressure produces a finer mist, which cools more quickly. Suppliers recommend placing the nozzles about 2 feet apart around the perimeter of the greenhouse, between the wall and the benches. Place the nozzles underneath the benches so the mist doesn't drench the plants. As with watering, avoid misting late in the day. Wet leaves and cold, humid air can encourage disease.

Lighting

The most basic greenhouses use only the sunlight nature provides to grow plants in a warmer environment than the plants would experience outdoors, but a greenhouse can be much more than that. If you're willing and able to run power to the structure—or if it's connected to your home—you can add lights that will not only extend growing days and growing seasons but will also allow you to care for your plants after dark. In fact, supplemental artificial lighting is key to turning a two- or three-season greenhouse into a four-season garden structure.

Supplementing natural light with artificial light can be tricky. Natural light is made up of a spectrum of colors that you can see (the red, orange, yellow, green, blue, indigo, and violet colors of the rainbow) and those you can't see (infrared and ultraviolet). Plants absorb light from the red and blue ends of the spectrum—blue light promotes plant growth; light from the red end of the spectrum encourages flowering and budding. The red-blue light combination is easily achieved when the source is the sun but a little more difficult when you're using artificial lighting. Intensity is also important: Lights that are set too far away or that don't provide enough brightness (measured in lumens or foot-candles) will produce weak, spindly plants.

The three types of light bulbs used in greenhouses are incandescent bulbs, fluorescent tubes, and high-intensity discharge (HID) lights, which include metal halide (MH) or high-pressure sodium (HPS). Each has advantages and disadvantages, which is why greenhouse gardeners often use a combination of two or more types to achieve light that is as close to natural as possible.

Incandescent
Ordinary tungsten incandescent bulbs are inexpensive, readily available, and a good source of red rays, but they are deficient in blue light. They can be useful for extending daylight for some plants and for supplementing low light levels, but they are not an efficient primary source of light. Incandescent lights produce a lot of heat—hanging them too close to plants can burn foliage, but if you hang them at a safe distance, they don't provide enough intensity for plant growth. The average life span of an incandescent bulb is about 1,000 hours.

Fluorescent
Fluorescent tubes are more expensive than incandescent bulbs, but the higher cost is amply offset by their longevity and efficiency: bulb life for

The right lighting in a greenhouse increases the number of hours you can work in the structure each day and expands the growing season and growing hours of plants.

Fluorescent is a better source of growth-stimulating light for your greenhouse. It must, however, be hung relatively close to plants in order to spur growth.

Ordinary incandescent lights aren't particulary good sources of growth-promoting light, but they can help heat a greenhouse. And their attractive warm light also turns a greenhouse into a nighttime landscape design feature.

fluorescents is about 10,000 hours, and they provide the same amount of light as incandescents with only one-quarter to one-third the amount of energy. They also produce much less heat than incandescent bulbs.

Fluorescent bulbs (or "lamps," as they're called by the lighting industry) come in a variety of colors and temperature ranges, including full-spectrum light. Cool white lamps, which produce orange, yellow-green, blue, and a little red light, are the most popular choice. To provide seedlings and plants with a nearly full spectrum of light, many growers combine one cool white lamp and one soft (or warm) white lamp in the same fixture.

Due to their energy efficiency and low heat output, fluorescent-tube fixtures are great for ambient lights that you might leave running for long periods, as well as for task lighting. They're also the best all-around choice for starting seedlings and growing small plants. The downside to using fluorescents as grow lights is that they must be hung very close to the plant—from 2 to 8 inches, depending on the plant—to be effective. This makes them most useful for propagation and low-growing plants.

HID

High-intensity discharge (HID) lights work by sending an electrical charge through a pressurized gas tube. There are two types: high-pressure sodium (HPS), which produces light in a narrow yellow-orange-red band, and metal halide (MH), which produces a broader range of light waves but tends to be more toward the white-blue-violet end of the spectrum.

Novice growers tend to use metal halide lights if they're using grow lights at all. But more experienced greenhouse gardeners, and those who grow throughout the year, may use a combination: MH lights to start plants off and encourage early growth and bushiness, then switching to HPS as the plants mature, because HPS light encourages flowering and fruiting. In fact, although most fixtures do not allow for bulbs to be interchanged, convertible fixtures are available that do allow the gardener to switch between bulbs.

HID lights of both types are very expensive, but they last a long, long time. A standard 400-watt HID bulb can provide 20,000 hours of lighting. These bulbs also light a large area: that single bulb will provide enough light for 16 square feet of plants. HID lights do, however, produce a good amount of heat. Hang them high in the greenhouse, and provide plenty of ventilation in warmer months.

LED Grow Lights

As lighting technology continues to evolve, light-emitting diodes (LEDs) are growing in popularity and use. Manufacturers have developed special LED grow lights that include both blue and red light waves, effectively serving all the needs of plants—from initial growth through mature budding, flowering, and fruiting. The big bonus of these bulbs is that they last almost as long as HID lights do but cost a fraction of the price. The lights can be used with conventional fixtures and provide wide, diffuse illumination that prevents the light from ever burning plant leaves.

Heating

Novice greenhouse gardeners can gain knowledge and extend their growing season with a basic lean-to or tiny kit greenhouse. But if you're going to take advantage of the full potential inherent in greenhouse gardening, you'll need to heat the greenhouse. There are several ways to do that. Some techniques, such as using a heat sink, are usually meant as a complement to a main heat source. In any case, the most common and simplest way to heat your greenhouse is with a heater. The two main types are electric and fuel fired (gas, propane, kerosene, or oil).

Electric heaters are inexpensive and easy to install. They provide adequate heat for a small greenhouse in a temperate climate and are useful for three-season greenhouses. However, they are expensive to operate (although relative costs are constantly changing) and do not provide sufficient heat for use in cold regions. Electric units can also distribute heat unevenly, making it too warm in some areas of the greenhouse and too cold in others. Placing a heater at each end of the greenhouse can help. If you use an electric heater,

be sure the fan doesn't blow warm air directly on the plant leaves; they may scorch.

Gas heaters usually cost more than electric and most areas require that a licensed professional hook them up, but heating bills will be lower than if you use an electric heater. Gas heaters operate much like a furnace: a thermostat turns on the heat when the temperature drops below its setting. You can help to distribute the heat by using a fan with the heater. If you plan to use a gas heater, install the gas line when you're building the foundation. It is also important to ensure that the heater is vented to the outside and that fresh air is available for combustion. Poor ventilation can cause dangerous carbon-monoxide buildup.

Propane, oil, and kerosene heaters also need to be vented, and if you're using kerosene, be sure it's high-grade. Another option is hot-water heating, in which the water circulates through pipes set around the perimeter of the greenhouse under the benches. You can also consider overhead infrared heat lamps and soil-heating cables as sources of heat.

In most climates, an electric heater with an automatic thermostat will be sufficient to protect tender plants on cold nights. Electricity is an expensive heating option, however, so it's best reserved for moderate heating needs.

A portable space heater may be all the supplemental heat your greenhouse requires. Use it with caution, and make sure yours shuts off automatically if it overheats or is knocked over.

Calculating Heat Needs

Heat is measured in British thermal units (Btu), the amount of heat required to raise one pound of water 1 degree Fahrenheit. To determine how many Btu of heat output are required for your greenhouse, use the following formula.

Area (the total square footage of the greenhouse panels) × difference (the difference between the coldest nighttime temperature in your area and the minimum nighttime temperature required by your plants) × 1.1 (the heat-loss factor of the glazing; 1.1 is an average) equals Btu.

Calculate the area by multiplying the length by the height of each wall and roof panel in the greenhouse and adding up the totals. Here's an example, using 380 square feet for the greenhouse area and 45 degrees Fahrenheit as the difference between the coldest nighttime temperature (10 degrees Fahrenheit) and the desired nighttime greenhouse temperature (55 degrees Fahrenheit). 380 square feet × 45 × 1.1 = 18,810 Btu.

If the greenhouse is insulated or uses double-glazed glass or twin-wall polycarbonate, you can deduct 30 percent from the total Btu required; if it's triple-glazed, deduct 50 percent. You can deduct as much as 60 percent if the greenhouse is double-glazed and attached to a house wall.

HEATING REQUIREMENTS

- Heaters must be equipped with an automatic shut-off switch.

- Position several thermometers at bench level throughout the greenhouse so you can check that heat is evenly distributed.

- Do not place thermometers or thermostats in direct sunlight.

- Install an alarm to warn you if the temperature drops dangerously low. Set the temperature warning high enough to give you time to remedy the problem before plants die.

- Use a backup generator to supply power to electric heaters during power outages.

Oil, gas, kerosene, and other fuel-operated heaters must be vented to the outside and have a source of fresh air for combustion.

Conserving Heat

On cold, cloudy days and at night, solar heat is lost. Even if you have supplemental heating, holding onto that heat is essential to maintaining an optimal climate. Insulating the greenhouse and making use of heat sinks are the most effective means of conserving heat, but don't overlook heat thieves such as cracks and gaps. Be sure the glazing is tight, and seal any opening that lets in cold air.

If you built a concrete foundation, it may have polystyrene board installed between the concrete and the soil. Concrete rapidly loses heat if the ground around it is cold, and polystyrene insulation helps to reduce this heat loss. You can use polystyrene board or bubble insulation (similar to bubble wrap used for shipping) to temporarily insulate the walls of the greenhouse. Simply attach the material to the greenhouse frame beneath the benches before winter and remove it in the summer. You can also insulate the greenhouse from the outside. Plant low-growing plants around the foundation, or prop hay bales or burlap bags filled with dry leaves against the walls.

Heat Sinks

Heat sinks absorb solar energy during the day and radiate it back into the greenhouse at night. Stone, tile, and brick floors and walls are good collectors of heat, but to be really effective, they should be insulated from underneath. Piles of rocks can act as heat sink, but the best option is a blue- or black-painted barrel or drum full of water. Place a few of them around the greenhouse. If you have an attached greenhouse, painting the house wall a dark color can cause it to radiate solar heat back into the greenhouse at night. A light-colored wall, on the other hand, can help reflect heat and light back into the greenhouse during the day.

This heat sink system uses solar energy to heat the greenhouse. Air heated by the sun is drawn in by the fan and blown into the rock pile, which also absorbs solar heat. Heat is radiated back into the greenhouse after the sun goes down.

SMART HEAT CONSERVATION

- Reduce the temperature by 5°. Growth may be slowed, but plants will survive.

- Make sure the greenhouse is as airtight as possible.

- To prevent drafts, add a storm door.

- Mulch the soil in raised benches to insulate it during cool seasons. Consider watering tropical foliage plants and other warm-season plants with water warmed to 65°F.

- Insulate all water- or steam-heating supply lines.

- At night, hang black cloth horizontally from the greenhouse ceiling as close to the plants and benches as possible to prevent the warm air from escaping through the roof.

- If the greenhouse uses automatic vents that are controlled by a separate thermostat, set that thermostat 5° or 10° higher than the heater thermostat to keep the vents from opening when the heat is on.

- Install an alarm system that will go off when the temperature goes above or below the safe range or when there is a power failure.

- Make use of the heat exhausted by your clothes dryer by running the vent into your greenhouse.

- Plant a "shelter belt" of evergreens on the windward side of the greenhouse to reduce heating costs. (But be sure it is far enough away that it doesn't cast shade on the greenhouse.)

MICROCLIMATES

When you landscape your property, you consider its microclimates: the sunny, sheltered corner; the cool, shady spot beneath the trees; that strip along the back that always catches the breeze. Your greenhouse has microclimates, too. It's warmer near the roof and cooler at floor level; some spots are shaded and others receive strong, direct light; and down near the wall vents, it's cool and breezy. Like the plants in a garden, greenhouse plants have differing light, heat, soil, and moisture requirements. Before you place them in the greenhouse, take stock of the microclimates, and group plants according to their needs.

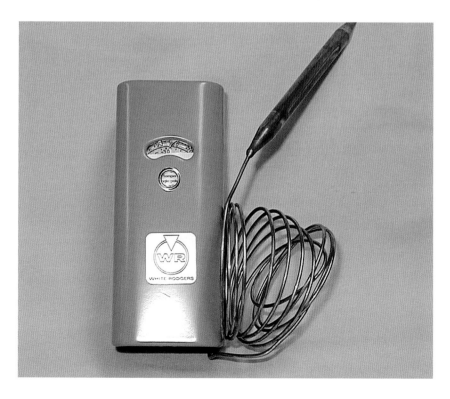

A heating and cooling thermostat is perhaps the most important greenhouse control device. The thermostat will control heat sources and automatic ventilaters to cool the greenhouse when temperatures climb into the danger zone for overheating plants.

Ventilation

Whether your plants thrive depends on how well you control their environment. Adequate sunlight is a good start, but ventilation is just as important. It expels hot air, reduces humidity, and provides air circulation, which is essential even during winter to move cold, stagnant air around, keep diseases at bay, and avoid condensation problems. You have two main options for greenhouse ventilation: vents and fans.

Because hot air rises, roof vents are the most common choice. They should be staggered on both sides of the ridgeline to allow a gentle, even exchange of air and proper circulation. Roof vents are often used in conjunction with wall vents or louvers. Opening the wall vents results in a more aggressive air exchange and cools the greenhouse much faster than using roof vents alone. On hot days, you can open the greenhouse door to let more air inside. Also consider running small fans to enhance circulation.

Vents can be opened and closed manually, but this requires constant temperature monitoring, which is inconvenient and can leave plants wilting in the heat if you are away. It's far easier—and safer—to use automatic vent openers. These can be thermostat-controlled and operated by a motor, which turns on at a set temperature, or they can be solar-powered. Unlike thermostat-controlled vent openers, which require electricity, solar-powered openers use a cylinder filled with wax, which expands as the temperature rises and pushes a rod that opens the vent. When the temperature drops, the wax shrinks and the vent closes. How far the vent opens is dictated by temperature: the higher the temperature, the wider the vent opens to let in more air.

A fan ventilator is a good idea if you have a large greenhouse. The fan is installed in the back opposite the greenhouse door, and a louvered vent is set into the door wall. At a set temperature, a thermostat mounted in the middle of the greenhouse activates the fan, and the louvered vent opens. Cool air is drawn in through the vent, and the fan expels the warm air. The fan should be powerful enough to provide a complete air exchange every 1 to 1.5 minutes.

CALCULATING VENTILATION REQUIREMENTS

Greenhouse manufacturers rarely include enough vents in kits, so be sure to buy more. To determine the square footage of venting your greenhouse should have, multiply the square footage of the floor by 0.2.

Automatic openers sense heat buildup and open vents. Some openers are controlled by standard thermostats, while others are solar-powered.

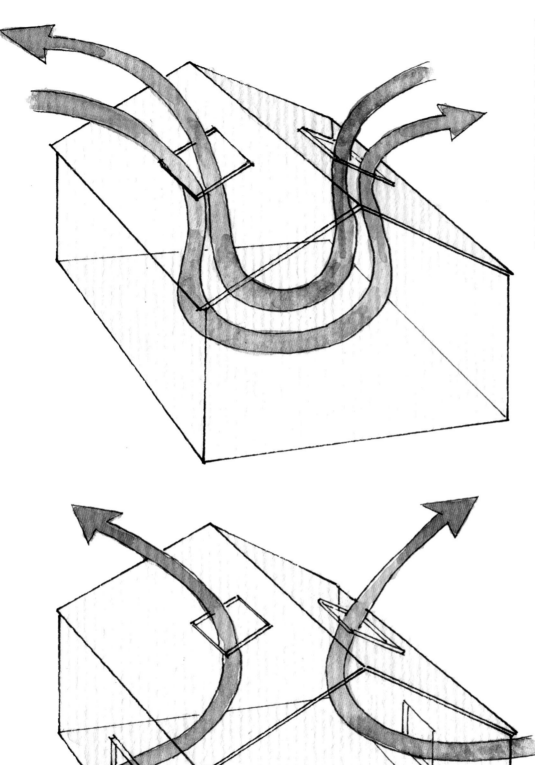

Venting your greenhouse–
Installing at least one operable roof vent on each side of the ridgeline creates good air movement within the structure. Adding lower intake vents helps for cooling. Adding fans to the system greatly increases air movement.

Cooling

Although vents and fans are the first line of defense when the temperature inside the greenhouse starts to climb, other cooling methods such as misting, humidifying, evaporative cooling, and shading can also help to maintain the ideal growing environment. Cooling is crucial during summer, but it can be just as important on a sunny winter day.

Shades

By blocking direct sunlight, shades protect plants from sunburn and prevent the greenhouse from getting too hot. They can be installed on the exterior or hung from cables inside the greenhouse. Both methods block the sun, but only exterior shades prevent solar energy from penetrating the glazing, thereby keeping the air inside the greenhouse cooler.

When choosing shades, be sure they are UV stabilized for longevity.

Two types of shades are available: cloth and roll-up. Shade cloth is usually woven or knitted from fiberglass or polyethylene and is available in many colors, although green, black, gray, and white are most common. You can also find shade cloth in silver, which, like white, reflects heat and sunlight and keeps the greenhouse cooler than darker colors. Shade cloth also varies in density, usually from 20 percent to 80 percent. The higher the density of the cloth, the more light it blocks (60 percent density blocks 60 percent of the light). Be careful when choosing shade density; too little light will slow plants' growth.

Shade cloth can be simply thrown over the greenhouse and tied down when shading is needed, but this hampers airflow through the vents (unless you cut the cloth to size and install it in sections). Better ventilation is achieved by suspending the cloth 4 to 9 inches above the exterior glazing. Be sure the vents are open when you do this. Greenhouse shade suppliers can provide framework kits.

GREENHOUSE SHADING COMPOUND

Professional greenhouse growers with large operations typically apply greenhouse shading compound to the glazing of their structures so they can control heat entry and protect their plants. Similar to paint, shading compound contains ground pigments that reflect the sun's rays. The compound is sprayed onto the glazing with an airless sprayer (you can use a hand-sprayer for a small greenhouse). Sold in 5-gallon buckets, it is diluted with water at an 8 to 1 ratio for plenty of coverage. Some types are designed to be easily removed with water and a fine nylon broom so you can make adjustments as needed. Other formulations are intended to be permanent. For more information, ask about the product at your greenhouse supply store or do an online search for Greenhouse Shading Compound.

Roof shades, along with vents, help prevent a greenhouse from overheating in direct sunlight. Here, a combination of circulating fans and cloth shades mounted on the interior of the south-facing glass helps protect plants.

Louvered and roll-up shades help to block the sun in this greenhouse.

In addition to cloth, roll-up greenhouse shades may be constructed from aluminum, bamboo, or wood. They are convenient because you roll them up when they're not needed, and they last longer than shade cloth, but they are more expensive.

Evaporative Coolers

Evaporative coolers (also called swamp coolers) cool the air by using a fan to push or pull air through a water-saturated pad. A portable cooler might be sufficient for a small greenhouse; larger greenhouses will benefit from a unit cooler placed outside. Used when the humidity outside is less than 40 percent, these units draw dry outside air through the saturated pad, where it is cooled. The air travels through the greenhouse and exits via a vent on the opposite side. It's a good idea to use an algaecide with these coolers.

Liquid Shading

Some greenhouse gardeners choose to paint liquid-shading compounds (sometimes called whitewashing) over the outside glazing. These compounds are inexpensive and easy to apply, but they can be unattractive and tend to wash off in the rain. Liquid shading can be thinned or layered to the level desired, and the residue can be brushed off at the end of summer. (It is often almost worn off by that point anyway.) Some liquid-shading compounds become transparent during rainy weather to let in more light and then turn white when they dry.

Roof vents that are triggered to open automatically by sensor alerts are far and away the most important component of a greenhouse cooling system. But additional cooling devices may be necessary.

Workbenches & Storage

Almost any greenhouse can benefit from the right workbench in the right area. But choose carefully, because the weight and messiness of some plants means only certain workbenches will do.

How you lay out benches depends on your needs and the size of your greenhouse. Most average-size greenhouses can accommodate a bench along each wall, with an aisle down the middle for access. If you have enough space along one endwall, you can install more benches to create a U shape. Another option is to arrange the benches in a peninsula pattern. Shorter benches are set at right angles to the outside walls, with narrow aisles in between, leaving space for a wider aisle down the middle. You can also use a single, wider bench along a side wall and leave space for portable benches and taller plants against the other wall. A larger greenhouse can accommodate three benches with two aisles.

Regardless of the layout you choose, it's best to run workbenches east to west so plants receive even light distribution throughout the day. Use the space as efficiently as possible, and don't inadvertently block the door. Allow enough room in the aisles to move around comfortably; make them wider if you need to accommodate a garden cart or wheelbarrow. Set benches about 2 inches from the greenhouse walls to provide airflow, and avoid placing benches near any heat source.

Bench width is determined by the length of your reach, so if you are short, you may want benches to be narrow. The same concept applies to height: although the average bench is about 28 to 32 inches, yours can be higher or lower to suit your height and reach. (If they need to be wheelchair-accessible, lower them even more.) If you have access to benches from both sides, you can double their width.

Several options are available for bench tops. Wood slats are sturdy and attractive, and they provide good drainage and airflow. Use pressure-treated or rot-resistant wood, such as cedar, keeping in mind that cedar benches can be expensive. Wire mesh costs less, is low-maintenance, and also provides good airflow, but be sure that it is strong enough to support heavy plants. Plastic-coated wire-mesh tops are available. These are similar to (if not the same as) the closet shelving found in home stores. Usually white, they have the advantage of reflecting light within the greenhouse.

Sturdy benches that are easy to clean and withstand moisture are a critical part of a greenhouse that's pleasant to work in.

For space efficiency, potting benches can double as storage containers. Here, the potting benches include spaces for mixing and storing soils for potting. Slatted covers make it easy to keep the bench-tops tidy.

You can also choose solid tops made of wood, plastic, or metal. Solid wood tops should be made from pressure-treated wood, and metal tops should be galvanized to prevent rust. Solid tops provide less air circulation than slatted or mesh tops, but they retain heat better in winter and are necessary if you use a capillary-mat watering system.

The greenhouse framing material will determine whether you can install shelves. Shelves can easily be added to a wood-framed greenhouse, and many aluminum greenhouse kit manufacturers provide predrilled framing, along with optional accessories for installing shelves. Keep in mind that even if shelves are wire mesh, they can cast shade onto the plants below.

If you plan on potting inside the greenhouse, you can use part of the benches or dedicate a separate space for a potting bench in a shady corner or along an endwall. For convenience, consider building or buying a potting tray that you can move around and use as needed.

Unless you have a separate place to store tools and equipment, you'll need to find room for them in the greenhouse. To determine how much space you'll need, first list all of the equipment necessary to operate the greenhouse: everything from labels, string, and gardening gloves to bags of soil, pots, trash cans, and tools. If you will use harmful chemicals, be sure to include a lockable storage area.

Just as in your home, finding storage space in the greenhouse can be a challenge. Look first to shady areas. If the greenhouse has a kneewall, the area under the benches can provide a good deal of storage space. Shelves can also provide storage space for lightweight items. Be creative and make efficient use of any area where plants won't grow to create accessible yet tidy storage for equipment.

Potting Materials

If you're a container gardener, you are already familiar with the vast array of pots available at garden centers. For greenhouse gardening, however, pot choices are narrowed to two types: terra cotta and plastic.

Terra cotta pots are attractive and heavier than plastic, which means they are less likely to be knocked over. In addition, they are porous—because water evaporates through the clay, the risk of overwatering is lower. However, you will have to water plants more often and clean the pots regularly to remove deposits caused by minerals from water and soil leaching through the sides. Glazed terra cotta pots hold moisture better than unglazed pots and don't show mineral deposits. Terra cotta pots are more expensive than plastic pots.

Practical and inexpensive, plastic pots hold moisture better than terra cotta pots, so you don't have to water plants as often. Gardeners who plan to start seeds and propagate plants often use plastic trays, flats, and cell packs, although peat pots, cubes, and plugs are also available for starting seeds.

Terra cotta containers are preferable if your plants will live in the pot permanently. If you are only starting plants for transplant, inexpensive plastic pots and trays are a good choice.

Hydroponics, the process of growing plants without soil, has become popular with greenhouse gardeners, especially for growing vegetables. Hydroponic growing medium, which holds plants in place, can be made of polystyrene balls, expanded clay pellets, gravel, pea stone, perlite, vermiculite, rock wool, or coconut fibers. The simplest method is to place growing medium into a pot and add a nutrient solution once or twice a day. A more complex system involves using computer-controlled pumps to automatically flush plants' roots with nutrient solution as necessary for maximum growth.

Lettuces are probably the most common hydroponically grown vegetable. They often are shipped with the root system intact for greater longevity.

Root systems grow through the plant support medium and down into the water below. Here, the water is contained in a child's plastic wading pool.

Many vegetables and herbs that are suitable for greenhouse growing are also good candidates for a hydroponic environment. Testing different species and judging their success can be a fun process.

Easy-to-Build Greenhouses

Some greenhouse designs are so simple that construction requires only a weekend or two. The foundation can be an anchored wooden frame or, for a more permanent structure, a concrete base.

Hoophouse

Economical and versatile, a hoop-style greenhouse (also called a hoophouse or a quonset house) is constructed of PVC or metal pipes that are bent into an inverted U shape, attached to a base, and connected at the top by a ridgepole. A hoophouse is usually covered with plastic sheeting. A door can be set at one end, and there may be an exhaust fan or flap vent that can be rolled up for ventilation. Because the hoop greenhouse is lightweight, it is not a good choice in areas with strong winds. (For instructions on building a hoophouse, see pages 102 to 107.)

A-frame Greenhouse

An A-frame greenhouse is small and lightweight and can be made of wood or PVC. A series of A-frames is attached to a wood base and covered with plastic sheeting or rigid plastic panels, such as polycarbonate or fiberglass. Because of the steep pitch of the roof, this type of greenhouse easily sheds rain, snow, and leaves and provides more headroom than a hoop greenhouse. It can also be portable.

A hoophouse is a simple greenhouse made by wrapping clear plastic over a series of U-shape frames. See page 102.

An A-frame greenhouse is a structure that is both incredibly simple and very stable. It's a great starter option for novice greenhouse gardeners.

Greenhouse Kits

No matter what kind of greenhouse you have in mind, chances are you can find a kit to match your vision. Dozens of companies offer kits in diverse styles, sizes, materials, and prices. Some offer door options—sliding versus swinging doors, for example, with and without locks and screens. Some offer glazing combinations, such as polycarbonate roof panels with glass walls. And some even offer extension kits for certain models, so you can add onto your greenhouse as your space requirements grow.

Kit basics usually include framing, glazing panels, vents (though usually not enough—it's a good idea to buy extras), and hardware. A good kit will come predrilled and precut, so you only need a few tools to assemble it. Most kits do not include the foundation, benches, or accessories.

Be sure the kit you choose comes with clear, comprehensive instructions and a customer-service number for assistance. Also ensure that it complies with your local building codes and planning regulations. Depending on the company, shipping may be included in the price. Because kits are heavy, shipping can be expensive; be sure to figure it and the cost of the foundation, benches, all necessary accessories, and the installation of utilities into your budget.

This kit greenhouse has an aluminum frame and polycarbonate panels. It features sliding doors and a roof vent. With nearly 200 square feet of floor space, it was a good bargain at around $800. See page 94.

Cold Frames

An inexpensive foray into greenhouse gardening, a cold frame is practical for starting early plants and hardening off seedlings. It is basically a box set on the ground and topped with glass or plastic. Although mechanized models with thermostatically controlled atmospheres and sashes that automatically open and close are available, you can easily build a basic cold frame—or several, in a range of sizes (see page 178). Just be sure to make the back side of the frame about twice the height of the front so that the glazing can be slanted on top. Also ensure that the frame is tall enough to accommodate the ultimate height of the plants growing inside. The frame can be made of brick, plastic, wood, or other materials, and it should be built to keep drafts out and the soil in. Most important, the soil inside must be fertile, well tilled, and free of weeds.

If the frame is permanently sited, position it to receive maximum light during winter and spring and to offer protection from wind. An ideal spot is against the wall of a greenhouse or another structure. Ventilation is important; more plants in a cold frame die from heat and drought than from cold. A bright March day can heat a cold frame to 100 degrees Fahrenheit (38 degrees Celsius), so be sure to monitor the temperature inside, and prop up or remove the cover when necessary. On cold nights, especially when frost is predicted, cover the box with burlap, old quilts, or fallen leaves for insulation.

HOTBEDS

Similar in construction to cold frames (but not as common), hotbeds have been around since Roman times. Emperor Tiberius directed his gardeners to grow cucumbers in dung-filled carts that were wheeled outside during the day and brought into a rudimentary "greenhouse" at night so that he had a supply of the vegetables year-round. This type of garden incorporates horse or chicken manure, which releases heat as it decomposes. The manure is set within the bed frame below ground level and is then topped with a layer of soil. (If you prefer, you can forgo the manure and lay heating cables between soil layers.) To prevent overheating, ventilate a hotbed as you would a cold frame.

A prefabricated cold frame such as this offers many benefits, including an easy-to-use flip top, white plastic glazing that diffuses light, and an attractive appearance.

Sunrooms

A greenhouse can certainly satisfy the desire to grow a profusion of plants year-round, but it's not everyone's cup of tea. Even the most avid gardener will agree that operating and maintaining a greenhouse requires a major commitment—in a greenhouse, the plants depend solely on you for their well-being. The sunroom, on the other hand, allows you to surround yourself with flowers and plants in a sunny, light-filled room that is designed primarily for your comfort.

Like the greenhouse, the sunroom's roots are found in the orangeries and conservatories built on the grand estates of Europe. In the nineteenth-century conservatory, fashionable women gathered under the glass in exotic, palm-filled surroundings for tea. The twenty-first-century garden room invites us to do the same, in a comfortable interior environment from which we can appreciate the outdoors year-round.

Large windows and doors open onto the terrace or garden. A high roof, which might be all glass, lets in abundant natural light. Decorative architectural features announce that this place is different from the rest of the house—separate, but in harmony. Like the conservatories of old, sunrooms can be used for growing plants and flowers indoors, but they are just as often used as sitting rooms, from which to admire the plantings outside the windows.

The sunroom can be a grand conservatory—an ornamented, plant-filled glass palace attached to an equally grand home. Or it can be a modest room containing little more than a few potted plants and a comfortable reading chair. Grand or modest, the sunroom is neither wholly of the house nor of the garden; it is a link between the two, a place in which you can feel a part of the garden but with all of the comforts of home.

Like greenhouses, sunrooms can be as simple or as elaborate as your budget and style will allow. This sunroom blends beautifully with the house.

Greenhouse Styles

When choosing a greenhouse, consider the benefits and disadvantages of each style. Some offer better use of space, some better light transmission; others offer better heat retention, and some are more stable in strong winds. Keep in mind how you plan to use the greenhouse—its size and shape will have an impact on the interior environment.

Traditional Span

A Ventilating roof windows
B High gable peak provides headroom
C 45° roof angle encourages runoff
D Solid kneewalls block wind, provide impact protection, and allow insulation

This type of greenhouse has vertical side walls and an even-span roof, with plenty of headroom in the center. Side walls are typically about 5' high; the roof's central ridge stands 7 to 8' above the floor. This model shows a low base wall, known as a kneewall, but glass-to-ground traditional-span houses are also widely available. Kneewalls help to conserve heat but block light below the benches; glass-to-ground houses suffer more heat loss but allow in more light.

Lean-To

A Adjoining house provides structure and heat
B Aluminum frame is lightweight but sturdy
C Roof vents can be set to open and close automatically
D Well sealed door prevents drafts and heat loss

Because it is attached to the house, a lean-to absorbs heat from the home and offers easy access to utilities. This model shows curved eaves, a glazed roof, and glass-to-ground construction. Lean-tos can be built on kneewalls to provide more headroom and better heat retention than glass-to-ground styles. Sinking the foundation into the ground about 2 to 3' can conserve even more heat.

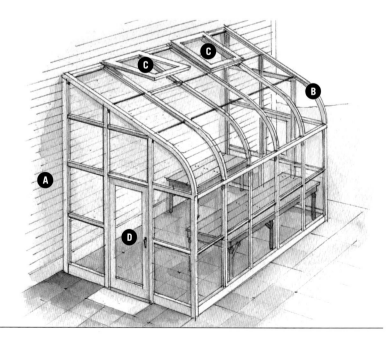

Three-Quarter Span

A Adjoining house provides shelter

B Half-lite door insulates but allows some light in

C Operating side vent

D Gable creates headroom

Also attached to the house, this type of greenhouse offers the benefits of a lean-to with even more headroom and better light transmission (though it offers less light than a freestanding model). Because of the additional framing and glazing, this style is more expensive to build than a traditional lean-to.

Dutch Light

A Tapered sidewalls encourage condensation to run off

B Lower side vent encourages airflow

C Tile floor retains heat

D Roof angle minimizes light reflection

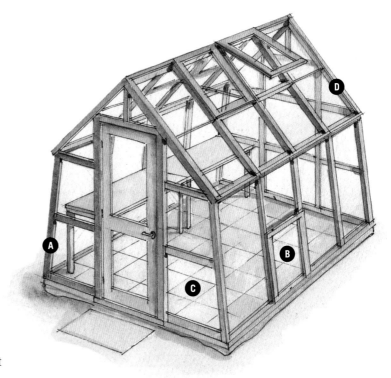

Especially suitable for low-growing border crops, such as lettuce, this design has sloping sides that allow maximum light transmission. However, the large panes of glass, which may be 30 by 59", are expensive to replace.

Mansard

A Full-width door frame
B Sliding doors can be adjusted
for ventilation
C Lower side vents encourage airflow
D Stepped angles ensure direct light
penetration any time of day or year

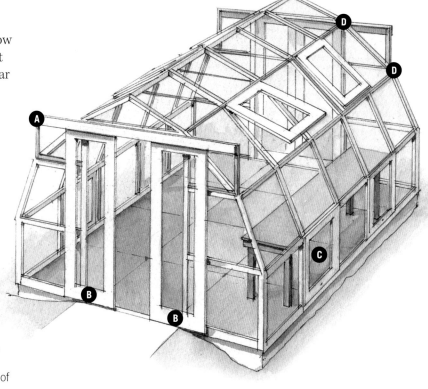

The slanting sides and roof panels that characterize the mansard are designed to allow maximum light transmission. This style is excellent for plants that need a lot of light during the winter.

Mini-Greenhouse

A Brick wall retains heat
B Upper shelf does not block airflow
C Full-depth lower shelf creates
hot spot below
D Full-lite storm door

A relatively inexpensive option that requires little space, this greenhouse is typically made of aluminum framing and can be placed against a house, a garage, or even a fence, preferably facing southeast or southwest, to receive maximum light exposure. Space and access are limited, however; and without excellent ventilation, a mini-greenhouse can become dangerously overheated. Because the temperature inside is difficult to control, it is not recommended for winter use.

Dome

A Geometric dome shape is sturdy and efficient
B Louvered air intake vent
C Gussets tie structure together
D Articulated door is visually interesting (but tricky to make)

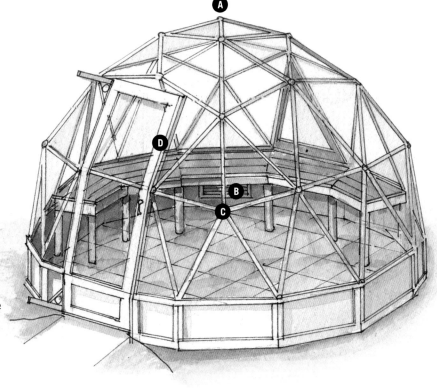

This style is stable and more wind-resistant than traditional greenhouses, and its multi-angled glass panes provide excellent light transmission. Because of its low profile and stability, it works well in exposed locations. However, it is expensive to build and has limited headroom, and plants placed near the edges may be difficult to reach.

Polygonal

A Triangular roof windows meet in hub
B Finial has Victorian appeal
C Built-in benches good for planters or for seating
D Lower wall panels have board-and-batten styling

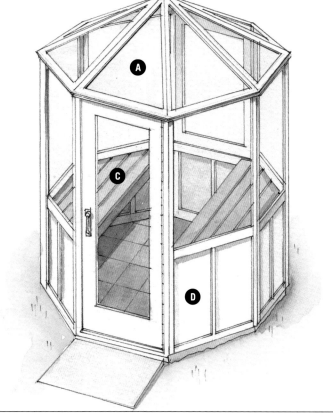

Though it provides an interesting focal point, this type of greenhouse is decorative rather than practical. Polygonal and octagonal greenhouses are typically expensive to build, and space inside is limited.

Alpine House

A Banks of venting windows at both sides of peak

B Adjustable louvers for air intake

C Cedar siding on kneewall has rustic appeal

D Fixed roof windows lend stability

Specifically designed for plants that normally grow at high elevations and thrive in bright, cool conditions, this alpine house is unheated and has plenty of vents and louvers for maximum ventilation. Doors and vents are left open at all times (except in winter). Many rock-garden plants—edelweiss, sedum, and gentian, for example—appreciate the alpine house environment.

Hoophouse

A Bendable PVC tubes provide structure

B 4-mil plastic sheeting is very inexpensive glazing option

C Roll-up door

D Lightweight base makes hoophouse easy to move

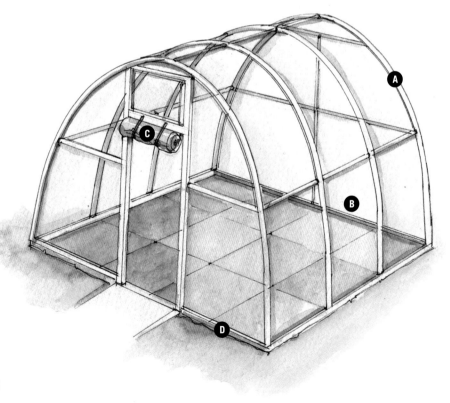

Made of PVC or metal framing and plastic glazing, this lightweight, inexpensive greenhouse is used for low-growing crops that require minimal protection from the elements. Because it does not provide the warm conditions of a traditional greenhouse, it is designed mainly for extending the growing season, not for overwintering plants. Ventilation in this style can be a problem, so some models have sides that roll up.

Conservation Greenhouse

A High peak for good headroom
B Louvered wall vents
C Sturdy aluminum framing
D Broad roof surface for maximum heat collection

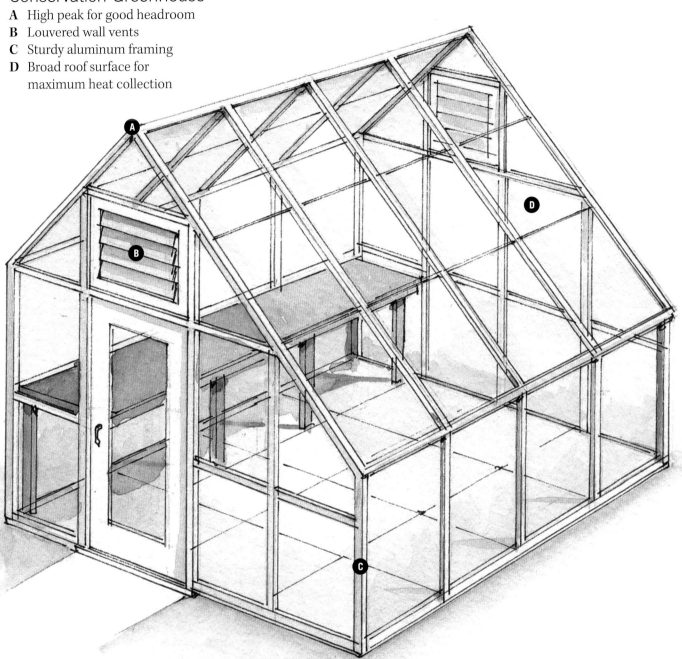

With its angled roof panels, double-glazing, and insulation, the conservation greenhouse is designed to save energy. It is oriented east-to-west so that one long wall faces south, and the angled roof panels capture maximum light (and therefore heat) during the winter. To gain maximum heat absorption for the growing space, the house should be twice as long as it is wide. Placing the greenhouse against a dark-colored back wall helps to conserve heat—the wall will radiate heat back into the greenhouse at night.

FREE GREENHOUSE DESIGN SOFTWARE

The United States Department of Agriculture (USDA) has developed a computer software program called Virtual Grower that you can use to create your own custom greenhouse design. It helps you make decisions about roof and sidewall materials, operating temperatures, and other variables. It even has a calculator for estimating heating costs. The software can be downloaded free of charge: https://www.ars.usda.gov/research/software.

Gallery of Greenhouses

For such a basic, utilitarian structure, there is an astounding diversity of greenhouse styles. Some are purely functional, while others are over-the-top gorgeous. That's why, once you've made all the practical decisions of how big it will be, where you'll put it, what services you'll need, and what foundation it will go on, you'll still have plenty of options to choose from based purely on looks.

The traditional glass greenhouse is giving way to modern versions with synthetic panels that are often opaque, diffusing light and sparing plant leaves from burning. But the forms of the greenhouse structure haven't really changed. You can choose a traditional gabled construction, a slant-sided Dutch style, or a thoroughly modern geodesic dome. You'll find a range of options covered in the pages that follow. Use these as inspiration for your ultimate decision.

Go grand when you want to marry traditional style to a stunning landscape. If money is no object, your greenhouse can be a jaw-dropping feature that creates a centerpiece for your landscape. This traditional greenhouse features a steel frame, glass glazing, and the time-honored roof crest that is not only a distinctive visual feature but also keeps birds from perching on the ridge and fouling the roof's panels.

Grow in modern style with a high-end prefab shed greenhouse. This backyard stunner is sold as a kit but looks custom. It includes operable vent windows, and the footprint lends itself to many different greenhouse workspace configurations. Keep in mind that a greenhouse can be a backyard focal point as well as a utility building.

The first order of business is always location, location, location. As the sun-drenched interior of this modern shed greenhouse shows, siting your greenhouse is the most important consideration. This one is located right in the middle of a backyard, avoiding shade from trees on the perimeter and taking advantage of the sun throughout the day.

Integrate your greenhouse. This Gothic arch-style structure is a trim and inoffensive addition to a yard, but it really comes into its own as a planned part of the landscape. Positioned at the end of a path with a raised bed behind it, it seems just as permanent as the wood arbor or brick walls in this large courtyard.

Start small with a lean-to. If you're not ready to commit to a full-blown greenhouse, a lean-to kit such as this one is a great way to get your feet wet. The simple construction belies a well-thought-out functionality. This kit comes with seals and gutters, and the homeowner has opted to create beds from mounded soil. Placing the lean-to on a brick patio meant that no foundation had to be dug.

Choose a lightweight option when you're not certain about siting. This well-constructed half-hoop kit greenhouse is a perfect starter for the novice gardener. It is easy to assemble and can be anchored in place or easily moved to a different location to suit different plants.

Consider hanging plants when choosing a framing material. Growing plants in hanging baskets lends another dimension to your greenhouse, but the framing has to be sturdy enough to support the additional weight. The solid wood rafter braces in this greenhouse are more than up to the job.

Look to kits for flexible options. This prefab Gothic arch-style greenhouse came complete with frame and panels as well as dual countertops that can be reconfigured to suit planting and work needs. Kit manufacturers also offer packages that include accessories such as the time and temperature control panels, thermostat, and vent fan in this greenhouse.

Maximize exposure with a geodesic dome greenhouse. This intriguing style makes the most of available sunlight and is excellent at counteracting wind and snow loads. The handsome kit shown here comes complete with a pony wall, polycarbonate panels, and all the hardware you'll need to build what is actually a fairly complex structure.

Build a stunning greenhouse with wood. Few materials are quite as handsome as wood when it comes to framing a greenhouse, and the redwood that makes up this frame is especially beautiful. Left untreated, the frame will age to an elegant gray. This is a prefab all-in-one structure, even though it looks custom built.

Integrate a kit greenhouse with other landscape features to make it seem at home. This tidy prefab unit is attractive enough with its crisp opaque panels, but it really seems part of the yard thanks to a bed planted next to it and planters around it.

Prep for greenhouse success. This is another Gothic arch-style prefab greenhouse that has been set up for longevity and efficiency. It sits on a framed foundation, with a dirt floor that can be used for growing and is forgiving of spills or accidents. The slotted benches are ready to hold plants in need of sun and tender care, and the stone path ensures slip-free accessibility in any season.

Think beyond growing when choosing your greenhouse. As this kit unit shows, a greenhouse can be a year-round relaxing room as well as a place to grow your favorite plants. It's all how you outfit it.

Play it safe with lean-tos. A subdued, attached greenhouse will fit attractively with your house. This white-framed prefabricated lean-to provides abundant space inside and looks integrated with the house—the glass, not the frame, dominates. A brick walkway wrapping around the lean-to adds to the appeal.

Seek details that aid construction— modern greenhouse manufacturers offer many construction shortcuts that make building your greenhouse easier. This framing connector alleviates the need for multiple miter cuts, shaving quite a bit of time off the construction process.

Outfit for what you want to grow. Orchids are finicky plants that require carefully curated growing conditions, and this greenhouse—equipped with a variable-speed direction fan, multiple vent windows, and a sturdy heater—makes the perfect home for them. It doesn't hurt that the gorgeous redwood frame is a beautiful complement to the showstopping flowers.

Find a frame color that will work with your location. This lovely kit greenhouse is offered in different frame colors, but the green here blends with the forest-like surroundings. In tandem with a custom-made platform, the frame and opaque panels create a very elegant visual.

Supplement greenhouses with the right portable cold frame. This trim, prefab unit can be used on a patio with potted plants or placed right over young plants in a bed. It's easy to clean, durable, and a great partner to a greenhouse in the garden.

Go big in a sun-drenched area. This sizeable "hobby" greenhouse offers plenty of room for plants of all types and plenty of window exposure to soak up the sun in a large, wide-open backyard.

Use a kneewall when appropriate. The solid kneewall around the bottom of this greenhouse makes the structure feel more rooted and permanent, and it also adds stability. The kneewall doesn't detract from sun exposure because nearby structures limit the sun to the upper portion of the greenhouses.

Keep climate in mind when choosing a greenhouse. Areas prone to snow, hail, or gale-force winds all present challenges. To ensure that your greenhouse stays standing, select one meant to stand up to the elements in your local climate. The geodesic dome greenhouse here was obviously a good choice for the anticipated snow load.

Pick accessories to make greenhouse gardening easy on yourself. The solar-powered automatic openers shown here make opening and closing vents and louvers one less thing you need to worry about. As the black probes are hit by increasing sunshine, they slowly trigger the opening devices, working in reverse when the sun goes down.

Determine quality by looking at the fine details. Inspect any prefab greenhouse for signs of quality construction. This quick-fit fastener makes assembly easier and less stressful, and it will ensure the long-term stability of the greenhouse.

Stage your greenhouse to make it a focal point and an incredible addition to your landscape. This smartly appointed prefab greenhouse, with its clean and sharp appearance, is shown to its best advantage by being centered on a raised foundation of crushed, colored gravel, bordered by scalloped stones.

Organize your greenhouse from the start to ensure the gardening experience is as pleasant and efficient as possible. This simple greenhouse includes a center stone path that makes wheeling materials and plants in and out a breeze. The deep, sturdy workbenches ensure that plants have ample room while still leaving space for the gardener to work.

Greenhouse Projects

Although building a greenhouse involves many of the same principles that go into building a larger structure, such as a house or a room addition, a greenhouse is a much simpler project. You can also choose to begin your greenhouse adventure with a modest unit, growing into a larger, more fully equipped version once you become familiar with the process of growing plants in a controlled, indoor environment.

The projects in this section will accommodate any need, whether you're just starting out or looking to graduate to a much bigger, more complex greenhouse. Have a small yard and want to stick with the basics?

Regardless of which project you choose, keep in mind that it's all about the plants. The greenhouse you build needs to serve the type of plants—and the stage of growth—you want for your garden. It must also be within your skills and energy to build, so you don't wind up with a half-finished structure come summer.

In this chapter:

Custom Victorian Greenhouse

One objection to most kit greenhouses is that they tend to have little going for them on the style front: a plain metal framework supporting clear panels. If you're looking for a greenhouse project that blends with the look and character of your home, your best bet is to design and build one yourself.

The custom greenhouse seen in this project is designed and scaled to fit lean-to-style against a south-facing wall on an 1890s-era Victorian house. The principal design details that make it blend are the kneewall, which uses the same narrow wood lapsiding as the house, and the custom windows and door, which feature an arch element that is also present in the house trim. At roughly 6 × 9 feet in floorplan, the greenhouse is on the small side. But a space-conserving built-in-bench helps the gardener who designed the greenhouse get maximum usage from this small space.

The glazing on the greenhouse is ¼-inch-thick clear polycarbonate (See Resources, page 236). The roof panels are also clear ¼-inch polycarbonate, but with a hollow twin-wall construction that resists shattering and limits condensation. The roof vents are operated by lift arms with integral thermometers. When the air temperature inside the greenhouse hits around 85 degrees, the vents pop open automatically. The windows and the door are custom-made by sandwiching polycarbonate panels between wood frames. To allow for movement of the materials, the frames are bolted together through oversized bolt holes. All but one of the windows are hinged on the tops so they can swing open to enhance ventilation.

The greenhouse seen here features a poured concrete slab that is set apart from the house by an isolation joint. The back wall studs and roof panels are not connected to the house either, thus the greenhouse is technically a freestanding structure. Gaps between the greenhouse and the house are covered with various flashings, each of which is connected to one of the structures only. This has several advantages: primarily, it allows the structure to move and shift slightly (thereby avoiding cracking of glazing and roof panels) as the soil conditions and temperature change. And if the structure is small enough and has adequate setback distance from your property lines, you likely will not need a building permit. If the greenhouse were connected to the house, you would be required to dig full frost footings, as well.

TOOLS & MATERIALS

Shovel	Pencil	Concrete	Piano hinges
Garden rake	Tape measure	J-bolts	Automatic window vent opener (optional)
Hand tamper	Circular saw	Post anchors	
Drill/driver	Jigsaw	Socket wrench	Bolts
Framing square	Power miter saw	Concrete nails or screws	Wood glue
Level	Pen	Skew joist hangers	8d finish nails
Concrete mixer	Drywall saw	Joist hanger nails	Exterior-rated butt hinges
Mallet	Sandpaper	Paint and paint brush	Door pulls and eyehooks
Float	Straightedge guide	Seaming strip	Door stop moldings
Sheet plastic	Compactible gravel	Pole barn screws	Garage door sweep
Powder-actuated tool	Deck screws (2½", 3")	Metal flashing	Silicone caulk
Clamps	Metal re-mesh	Roof vent covers	

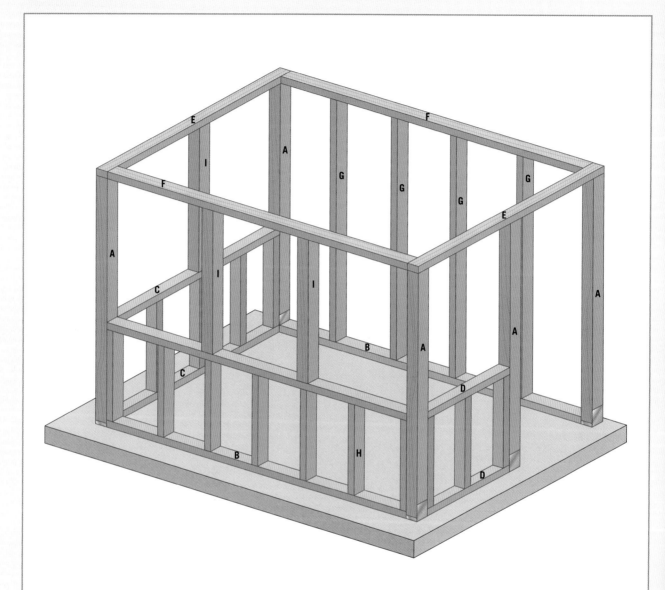

CUTTING LIST

KEY	PART	NO.	DIMENSION	MATERIAL
A	Post	5	$3\frac{1}{2} \times 3\frac{1}{2} \times 78"$	4×4
B	Front/back plate	2	$1\frac{1}{2} \times 3\frac{1}{2} \times 84\frac{1}{2}"$	PT 2×4
C	End plate	2	$1\frac{1}{2} \times 3\frac{1}{2} \times 56"$	PT 2×4
D	Door wall plate	2	$1\frac{1}{2} \times 3\frac{1}{2} \times 26"$	PT 2×4
E	End cap-bottom	2	$1\frac{1}{2} \times 3\frac{1}{2} \times 63"$	2×4
F	F/B cap-bottom	2	$1\frac{1}{2} \times 3\frac{1}{2} \times 84\frac{1}{2}"$	2×4
G	Back wall stud	4	$1\frac{1}{2} \times 3\frac{1}{2} \times 76\frac{1}{2}"$	2×4
H	Kneewall stud	15	$1\frac{1}{2} \times 3\frac{1}{2} \times 33"$	2×4
I	Upper stud	3	$3\frac{1}{2} \times 3\frac{1}{2} \times 42"$	4×4

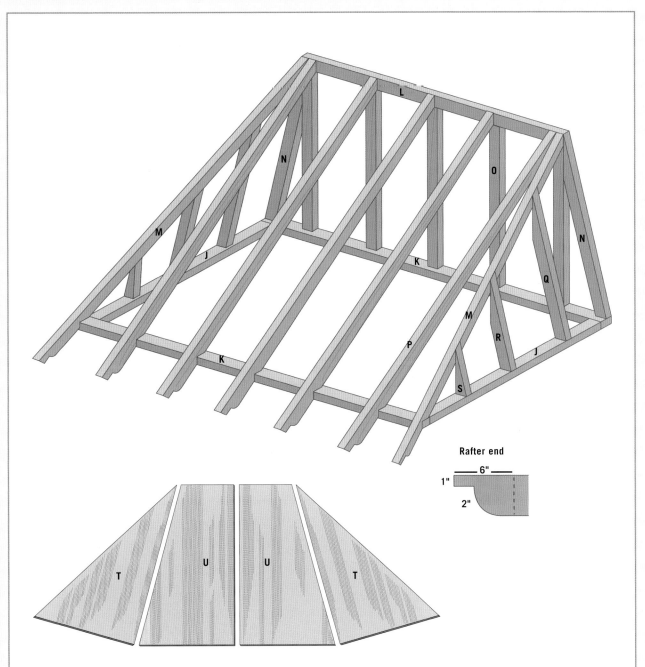

Rafter end

6"
1"
2"

CUTTING LIST

KEY	PART	NO.	DIMENSION	MATERIAL
J	End cap-top	2	1½ × 3½ × 56"	2 × 4
K	F/B cap-top	2	1½ × 3½ × 91½"	2 × 4
L	Roof ridge	1	1½ × 3½ × 64"	2 × 4
M	Skew rafter	2	1½ × 3½ × 79"	2 × 4
N	Roof leg	2	1½ × 3½ × 39½"	2 × 4
O	Roof support	5	1½ × 3½ × 34"	2 × 4

KEY	PART	NO.	DIMENSION	MATERIAL
P	Rafter	5	1½ × 3½ × 81"	2 × 4
Q	Cripple rafter	2	1½ × 3½ × 30"	2 × 4
R	Cripple rafter	2	1½ × 3½ × 22"	2 × 4
S	Cripple rafter	2	1½ × 3½ × 12"	2 × 4
T	Roof panel-side	2	¼ × 42 × 63"	Suntuf
U	Roof panel-main	2	¼ × 47 × 79"	Suntuf

WINDOW

CUTTING LIST (26 × 40½")

KEY	PART	NO.	DIMENSION	MATERIAL
W1	Rail-A	2	¾ × 3½ × 26"	1 × 4
W2	Stile-A	2	¾ × 3½ × 33½"	1 × 4
W3	Rail-B	2	¾ × 3½ × 19"	1 × 4
W4	Stile-B	2	¾ × 3½ × 40½"	1 × 4
W5	Insert	2	¾ × 5¼ × 19"	1 × 4
W6	Glazing	1	¼ × 26 × 40½"	Palsun

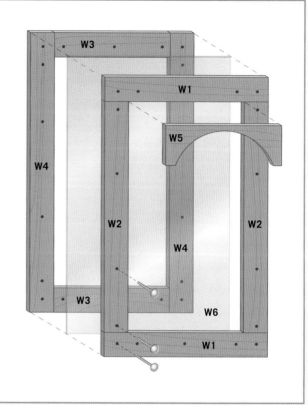

DOOR

CUTTING LIST (26 × 77½")

KEY	PART	NO.	DIMENSION	MATERIAL
D1	Rail-A	1	¾ × 3½ × 26"	1 × 4
D2	Rail-B	1	¾ × 5½ × 26"	1 × 6
D3	Rail-C	1	¾ × 3½ × 19"	1 × 4
D4	Rail-D	1	¾ × 5½ × 19"	1 × 6
D5	Stile-A	2	¾ × 3½ × 68½"	1 × 4
D6	Stile-B	2	¾ × 5½ × 77½"	1 × 4
D7	Insert	16	¾ × 5½ × 7¾"	1 × 6
D8	Glazing	1	¼ × 26 × 77½"	Palsun

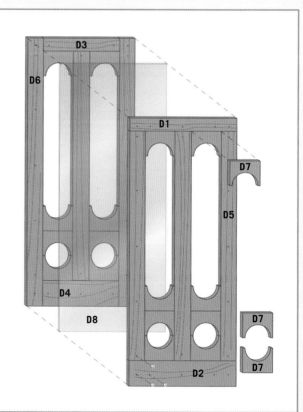

Materials for Building Custom Greenhouses

The glazing and roof panels in this custom greenhouse are made from ¼"-thick polycarbonate panels. The roof panels have vertical walls and are hollow, which makes them more dimensionally stable and less likely to crack than clear panels (a big benefit for roof). The ¼"-thick, clear polycarbonate used for the window and door glazing is very durable too. Standard ⅛"-thick clear acrylic can be used for roofs or glazing. It is relatively inexpensive and sold at most building centers. But it has a shorter lifespan than polycarbonate.

An automatic lifter arm contains a sensor that causes your roof window vents to raise when the interior temperature reaches a preset level—usually around 100°F.

Products for joining and fastening panels include a panel seam trim, which has wide flanges on both edges to accept two panels that butt together; 100% silicon caulk for sealing seams (check with the panel manufacturer for compatibility of adhesives and caulks); and rubber-gasket pole barn screws for fastening panels to rafters or purlins.

Stake out the installation area for the greenhouse. Strip off vegetation and then excavate for the subbase material and that portion of the slab you want to be underground. For drainage reasons, plan your slab so at least 1 to 2" of the concrete is above grade.

Install a 4 to 6" thick layer of compactible gravel to create a stable subbase. Tamp the gravel with a hand tamper or rental compactor. The tamped surface should slope away from the house at a very shallow rate—about ⅟₁₆" per foot. Insert an isolation board strip (usually made of asphalt-impregnated fiberboard) between the slab area and the foundation wall to keep the structures separate.

Build the three-sided concrete form and position it on top of the subbase. Screw the three 2 × 4s together with deck screws and then tack a 1 × 4 or 2 × 4 across the top, back ends of the sides. Square and level the forms and then drive wood stakes outside the 2 × 4 members. Attach the form to the stakes with deck screws driven through the stakes and into the form boards.

NOTE: The slab seen here is sized so there is a concrete apron of 2 to 3" around the structure, resembling a foundation wall. Some builders prefer to size the slab so the corner posts are flush with the slab edges, allowing you to cover the gap at the concrete surface with siding.

Add reinforcement in the concrete area. For most DIYers, metal re-mesh is an easy reinforcement material to work with. It is sold in 5 × 50' rolls and in 4 × 8' sheets. Prop the re-mesh on some small stones or bolsters. The edges of the reinforcement should be at least 4 to 6" away from the sides, and no closer than 1" to the concrete surface.

Pour concrete into the form. For a slab of the dimensions shown (4" thick by 68 × 84") approximately 15 cu. ft. (½ yard) of concrete is required (thirty 60-pound bags of dry mix). Settle the concrete by rapping the forms lightly with a mallet, and then strike off the material before floating.

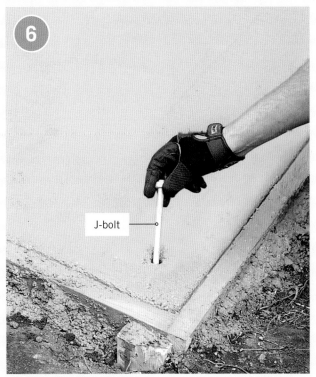

Set J-bolts into the concrete after it sets up and after you have rounded the edges with an edger tool. Make sure to follow your plan closely for the J-bolt positions. Cover the concrete with sheet plastic and allow it to dry overnight before removing the forms.

Install post anchors at the corners and at the doorjamb location. Standoff posts that elevate the post bottom slightly will greatly reduce the amount of water the post end will wick up from the footing.

Cut the 2 × 4 sill plates to fit between the posts, using pressure-treated lumber. Install the sill plates by fastening with a powder-actuated tool and concrete nails. Or, you can drill guide holes and install masonry anchor sleeves or simply drive concrete screws into the concrete. *(continued)*

Tack the posts in the standoff post bases with a couple of deck screws, making sure they are resting cleanly on the standoff pads. Also brace the posts with 2 × 4 braces so they are plumb. Tack all the posts in position and plumb them and then mark level cutting heights using a laser level or level for reference.

Remove the posts for trimming to final height, making sure to note which post belongs in which base. Marking and cutting in this manner ensures that the tops of all posts will be level even though the slab slopes away from the house. Precutting posts to the same length will result in a roof structure that is not flat. Reinstall the posts in the anchors and fasten with joist hanger nails or 16d galvanized nails.

Cut the 2 × 4 endwall cap plates to length and screw them to the tops of the corner posts with 3" deck screws. Test frequently to make sure the corners are square and the edges are flush with the post edges.

Clamp the doubled front and back wall cap plates together so the top plate overhangs the lower plate by 3½" on each end. Screw the top plates to the endwall cap plates and then fasten the front and back wall plates together with 2½" deck screws. Fasten the top cap plate on each end.

Build stud walls for the kneewalls between posts. Space the kneewall studs so they will be positioned beneath the intermediate posts. Attach cap plate to the tops of the studs.

Add 1 × 6 sills to the tops of the 2 × 4 kneewalls. The sills will cover the edges of the exterior siding, so make the interior edges flush with interior wall studs and cap plate.

Add intermediate 4 × 4 posts between the sills and the undersides of the doubled cap plates. These posts should be situated directly above kneewall studs. The posts are spaced so the distances between posts will create uniform-width bays for the windows.

Install back wall studs between the back sill plate and the back cap plates, spaced 16" on center. Do not attach these studs to the house—they must remain isolated from it structurally.

Construct and attach the roof ridge support wall, featuring a 2 × 6 on edge at the top of the wall. It is easiest to build this wall on the ground and then erect it as a unit. Use a pair of 2 × 4 braces to keep the support wall stable while you attach the rafters.   *(continued)*

Position a 2 × 4 so it spans from the ridge pole and past the header. Transfer cutting lines onto the workpiece and then cut the outer support legs to length at the marked angle. Attach the legs with deck screws.

Cut the rafters. Set workpieces in position against the 2 × 6 ridge pole and mark the point where they meet the header. Make a birdsmouth cutout in each rafter so it will rest flush on the header (top photo). Cut a decorative profile on each rafter end according to the Diagram on page 71 (bottom photo).

Install the corner rafters. First, attach skew joist hangers to the ends of the ridge pole for the skewed rafters that extend out to the front corners. Nail the rafters into the hangers with joist hanger nails. Toenail them (or drive screws toenail style) to the header.

Fill in the remaining rafters. If you wish, you can use joist hanger hardware to attach the rafters to the ridge pole. Or, you can nail or screw them. Spacing between rafters should be uniform.

Measure from the corner rafters to the endwall headers to find the lengths for the side rafters in the hip wall configuration. Cut 2 × 4 workpieces to length for each rafter.

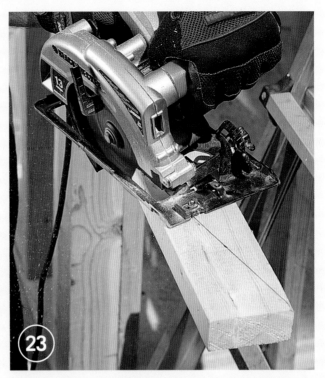

Clamp the side rafter workpieces to a sturdy worksurface and cut the top and bottom angles with a circular saw or jigsaw. The side rafters in this design do not overhang the wall headers. Attach the side rafters with screws driven through pilot holes.

Cut kneewall sheathing panels from exterior plywood and attach the panels to the kneewall studs with deck screws.

Cut and install trim boards and corner boards according to your plan for siding the kneewall. The tops of the trim boards should butt against the undersides of the sills.

(continued)

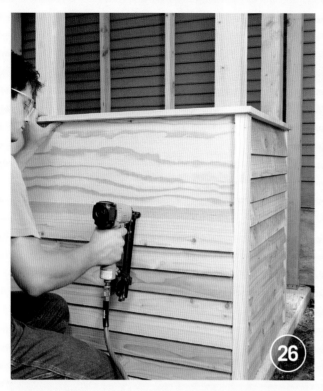

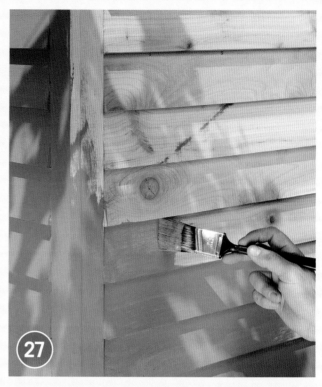

Install the siding on the kneewall. Generally, it is a good idea to install siding that matches the house siding. However, a well-chosen contrasting material also can have a pleasing design impact.

Paint the structure prior to adding roof panels and windows with glazing. Two coats of exterior paint is an adequate finish for an exterior lumber product, such as this cedar siding. A base coat of primer is always a good idea.

Seaming strip

Also seal the roof structure with paint before installing the roof panels. The charcoal colored paint seen here recalls the color of wrought iron, which was used frequently to construct greenhouses and related Victorian structures, such as orangeries.

Begin to fasten the roof panels. The twin-wall corrugated polycarbonate panels seen here are fastened directly to the rafters. A panel seaming strip with channels on each edge is fastened to the center rafter to create a transition between the two abutting panels. Install the strip first so you can take more accurate width measurements for cutting the panels.

Cut the first roof panel to rough size using a circular saw fitted with a fine-tooth panel-cutting blade. Use a straightedge cutting guide. Or, use a tablesaw if you have access to one.

Set one edge of the panel into the slot in the seam strip so it is in the exact position you'll install it. Use a marking pen to trace a cutting line onto the panel, flush with the edge of the endwall. Remove the panel and cut it to size.

Set the panel into position and test the fit.

 PROTECTING PANEL ENDS

Use foil tape to cover the top edges of corrugated panels, protecting the edges from moisture and insects (spiders love to lay eggs in channels like these). The edge on the bottom of the panel can be covered with foil tape also, but you'll need to poke a small weephole at the end of each channel so condensation can drain out. Or, you can use an alternate method such as L-shaped trim to protect the open panel ends (see Step 54).

(continued)

Fasten the roof panels with rubber-gasket equipped pole barn screws driven every 12" at each rafter or purlin. Take care not to overdrive the screws, but be sure they penetrate far enough to create a tight seal.

Cut the side roof panels to fit and attach them with rubber gasket screws. The hip seams will be covered with flashing (see page 83).

Frame openings for the roof vent cutouts. Install a pair of parallel framing members at the top and bottom of each opening. The tops of the frames should be flush against the roof panel.

Cut out the openings in the roof panels. Drill a starter hole at each corner and then use a drywall saw to make the cuts. Clean up the cut edges with sandpaper.

Install flashing over the hip roof seams. Here, common drip cap flashing is being fastened with rubber-gasket screws driven into the roof rafters.

Cover the gap between the standalone greenhouse structure and the house with metal flashing. Aluminum handy flashing (12" width) can be fastened to the house and lightly creased so it extends over the gap and forms a seal without any physical connection to the greenhouse.

Install roof vent covers. (Here, the installation of the covers was postponed to allow access through the vent holes for installing flashing.) Use a piano hinge to attach each roof vent cover to the roof.

Attach an automatic window vent opener to each roof vent cover, according to the hardware manufacturer's instructions. These devices have internal sensors that lift the vent cover when the greenhouse overheats. *(continued)*

Make the greenhouse windows. First, cut the window glazing panels (¼" clear polycarbonate is used here) using a circular saw and a straightedge guide. The glazing should equal the full height and width of the window. For convenience, this greenhouse was designed with all six windows exactly the same size.

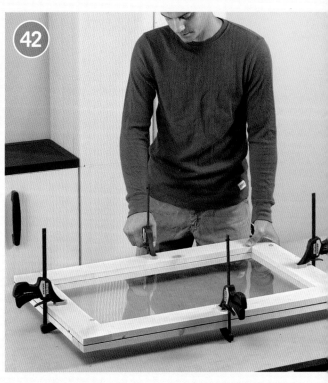

Cut the rails and stiles for the window frame to length from 1 × 4 pine stock. Assemble the frame parts around the glazing panel, clamping them together temporarily. Use the glazing panel as an alignment reference: if the panel is square and the frame edges are flush with the glazing all around, your window is square.

Drill guide holes for the bolts that draw the window parts together. Use a bit that's slightly larger than the diameter of the bolt shafts. This allows for slight expansion and contraction of the window parts as the temperature and humidity level change. Counterbore the bolt holes slightly.

Cut the arched inserts to fit at the top of the window frame opening. Install the inserts in the frame with glue and a couple of brads or pin nails. Install an insert on both the interior and the exterior sides of the window.

45

Install operable windows by centering the window unit in the opening, using shims to center it side-to-side and top-to-bottom. Hang the windows with exterior-rated pairs of butt hinges.

46

47

Attach door stop molding on the perimeter of each window opening, set so the window will be flush with the framed openings. Install fixed windows (if any) by centering the window unit in the opening side to side and driving a few 8d finish nails through pilot holes in the window and into the posts. Angle the pilot holes so the nail will not contact the glazing.

Install door pulls and eyehooks on the interior side of the window. Locate the pulls so they are centered and near the tops of the bottom window frame rails. Locate the eyehooks so there will be slight tension when the hook is in the screw eye—this will limit any rattling of the window.

48

49

Assemble the door frame. The center stiles should be attached to the frame rails with pocket screws or with deck screws driven toenail style. Clamp the parts together, sandwiching a piece of ¼" polycarbonate between the frames.

Bolt the door together in the same manner as the window, drilling over-sized guide holes and counterboring slightly for the nuts. Install two or three bolts in the center stile area to keep the frame and glazing from separating.

(continued)

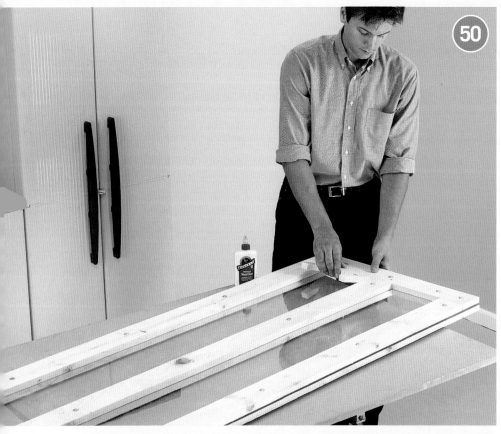

Cut the door panel inserts with a jigsaw and sand them smooth. Insert them into the framed openings as shown in the Diagram on page 72. Secure them on both sides of the glazing, using glue and brads or pin nails.

Hang the door. You may find it easier to paint it first. Door stop moldings should be installed so the door is flush with the outside greenhouse wall when closed. Add a latch and a handle. If you want to be able to lock the greenhouse, add a hasp and padlock.

Attach a garage door sweep (or comparable weatherstripping product) to cover the gaps between the greenhouse and the house. Flashing, such as drip cap, may be used to cover the gaps on the downsloping sides of the hip roof.

Make sure the foundation is clean and dry, then fill the gap between the concrete and the siding with clear silicone caulk.

Add trim elements to complete the roof. Parts of the roof trim system include: flashing over ridge (A); clear vent panel (B) attached with piano hinge (C) and automatic closer (D); seaming strip (E); metal drip cap for edges (F); ¼ × 1½" wood battens at rafter locations (G); vinyl cap molding at eave edges (H).

Finish the interior. You may add interior wallcoverings if you wish, but the exposed stud bays are good spots for adding shelving. For instructions on building this built-in potting bench, see pages 206 to 209.

DIY Gabled Greenhouse

Agreenhouse can be a decorative and functional building that adds beauty to your property. A greenhouse also can be a quick-and-easy, temporary structure that serves a purpose and then disappears. The wood-framed greenhouse seen here fits somewhere between these two types. The sturdy wood construction will hold up for many seasons. The plastic sheeting covering will last one to five seasons, depending on the materials you choose. It is easy to replace when it starts to degrade.

The 5-foot-high walls in this design provide ample space for installing and working on a conventional-height potting table. The walls also provide some space for plants to grow. For a door, this plan simply employs a sheet of weighted plastic that can be tied out of the way for entry and exit. If you plan to go in and out of the greenhouse frequently, you can purchase a prefabricated greenhouse door from a greenhouse materials supplier. To allow for ventilation in hot weather, we built a wood-frame vent cover that fits over one rafter bay and can be propped open easily.

You can use hand-driven nails or pneumatic framing nails to assemble the frame, if you wish, although deck screws make more sense for a small structure like this.

A wood-frame greenhouse with sheet-plastic cover is an inexpensive, semipermanent gardening structure that can be used as a potting area as well as a protective greenhouse.

TOOLS, MATERIALS & CUTTING LIST

(1) 20 × 50' roll 4- or 6-mil polyethylene sheeting

(12) 24"-long pieces of #3 rebar

(8) 8" timber screws

Compactable gravel (or drainage gravel)

Excavation tools

Level

Circular saw

Drill

Reciprocating saw

Maul

3" deck screws

Jigsaw

Wire brads

Brad nailer (optional)

Scissors

Utility knife

Tape measure

KEY	PART	NO.	DIMENSION	MATERIAL
A	Base ends	2	3½ × 3½ × 96"	4 × 4 landscape timber
B	Base sides	2	3½ × 3½ × 113"	4 × 4 landscape timber
C	Sole plates end	2	1½ × 3½ × 89"	2 × 4 pressure-treated
D	Sole plates side	2	1½ × 3½ × 120"	2 × 4 pressure-treated
E	Wall studs side	12	1½ × 3½ × 57"	2 × 4
F	Ridge support	1	1½ × 3½ × 91"	2 × 4
G	Back studs	2	1½ × 3½ × 76" *	2 × 4
H	Door frame sides	2	1½ × 3½ × 81" *	2 × 4
I	Cripple stud	1	1½ × 3½ × 16"	2 × 4
J	Door header	1	1½ × 3½ × 32"	2 × 4
K	Kneewall caps	2	1½ × 3½ × 120"	2 × 4
L	Ridge pole	1	1½ × 3½ × 120"	2 × 4
M	Rafters	12	1½ × 3½ × 60" *	2 × 4

Approximate dimension; take actual length and angle measurements on structure before cutting.

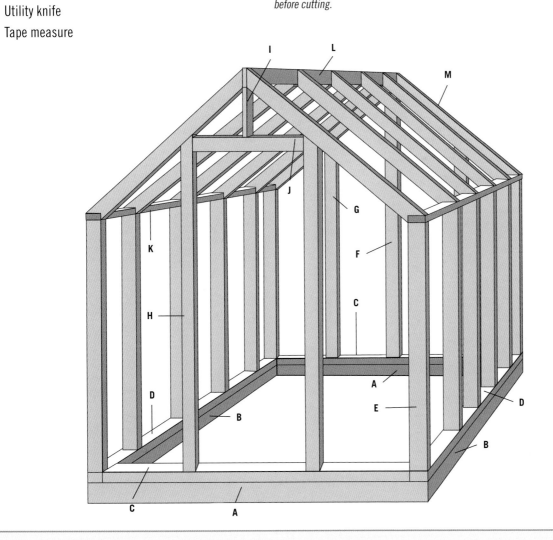

How to Build a Gabled Greenhouse

Prepare the installation area so it is flat and well drained (see page 74); then cut the base timbers to length. Arrange the timbers so they are flat and level and create a rectangle with square corners. Drive a pair of 8" timber screws at each corner, using a drill/driver with a nut-driver bit.

Cut 12 pieces of #3 rebar to length at 24" (if necessary), using a reciprocating saw or hacksaw. Drill a ⅜"-diameter pilot hole through each timber, near both ends and in the middle. Confirm that the timber frame is square by measuring diagonally between opposing corners (the measurements must be equal). Drive a rebar spike through each hole, using a hand maul, until the bar is flush with the timber.

Cut the sole plates, caps, and studs for the two kneewalls. Mark the stud layouts onto the plates and caps, spacing the studs at 24" on center. Assemble each kneewall by driving 3" deck screws through the sole plates and caps and into the ends of the studs.

Install the kneewalls onto the timber base. Set each wall onto a side timber so the sole plate is flush with the ends and side edges of the timber frame. Fasten the sole plate to the timber with 3" deck screws.

Begin the endwalls by cutting and installing the end sole plates to fit between the side plates, using 3" deck screws. Cut the ridge support posts to length. Toenail one post at the center of each end sole plate. Check the posts with a level to make sure they're plumb before fastening.

NOTE: The front post will be cut later to create the door opening.

Set the ridge pole on top of the support posts and check it for level. Install temporary cross braces between the outer wall studs and each support post, making sure the posts are plumb before fastening the braces. Double-check the posts and ridge for plumb and level, respectively.

Create a template rafter by cutting a 2 × 4 at about 66". Hold the board against the end of the ridge and the top outside corner of a wall cap. Trace along the face of the ridge and the cap to mark the cutting lines for the rafter. Cut along the lines, then test-fit the rafter and make any necessary adjustments for a good fit.

Mark and cut the remaining rafters, using the template to trace the cutting lines onto each piece of stock.

TIP: A jigsaw or handsaw is handy for making the bottom-end cuts without having to over-cut, as you would with a circular saw. *(continued)*

Install the rafters, using the deck screws driven at an angle into the kneewall caps and the ridge. The rafters should be aligned with the studs and perpendicular to the ridge.

Mark the two door frame studs by holding them plumb and tracing along the bottom edge of the rafter above. Position the studs on-the-flat, so the inside edge of each is 16" from the center of the support post (for a 32"-wide door, as shown). Install the studs with angled screws. Cut and install two studs on the rear endwall, spacing them evenly between the kneewalls and support post.

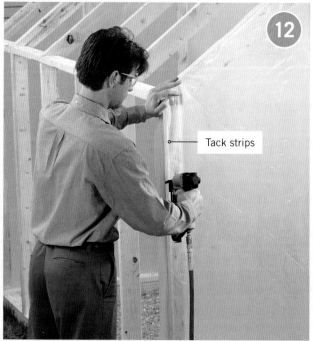

Tack strips

Complete the door frame: Mark the front support post 78" (or as desired) up from the sole plate. Make a square cut at the mark, using a circular saw or cordless trim saw (inset), then remove the bottom portion of the post. Cut the door header (from the post waste) to fit between the door studs. Fasten the header to the door studs and remaining post piece with screws.

Begin covering the greenhouse with the desired cover material (6-mil poly sheeting shown here), starting at the endwalls. Cut the sheeting roughly to size and secure it to the framing with wood tack strips fastened with wire brads. Secure the sheeting at the top first, the sides next, and the bottom last. Trim the excess material along the edges of the strips with a utility knife.

(13)

Attach sheeting to the edges of the sole plate on one side of the greenhouse, then roll the sheeting over the top and down the other side. Draw it taut, and cut it a little long with scissors. Secure the sheeting to the other sole plate (using tack strips), then attach it to the outside edges of the corner studs.

Door

2 × 4 weight

(14)

Create the door, using a piece of sheeting cut a little larger than the door opening (or purchase a door kit; see photo below). Secure the top of the door to the header with a tack strip. Weight the door's bottom end with a 2 × 4 scrap cut to length.

OPTION: Make a vent window. First, cut a hole in the roof in one rafter bay and tack the cut edges of the plastic to the faces (not the edges) of the rafters, ridge pole, and wall cap. Then build a frame from 1 × 2 stock that will span from the ridge to the top of the kneewall and extend a couple of inches past the rafters at the side of the opening. Clad the frame with plastic sheeting and attach it to the ridge pole with butt hinges. Install a screw-eye latch to secure it at the bottom. Make and attach props if you wish.

GREENHOUSE DOORS

Plastic door kits, available from greenhouse suppliers, include self-adhesive zipper strips and are easy to roll up and tie for access or ventilation. You can also create your own roll-up door with zipper strips and plastic sheeting purchased from a building center.

Freestanding Kit Greenhouse

Building a greenhouse from a prefabricated kit offers many advantages. Kits are usually very easy to assemble because all parts are prefabricated and the lightweight materials are easy to handle. The quality of kit greenhouses varies widely, though, and buying from a reputable manufacturer will help ensure that you get many years of service from your greenhouse.

If you live in a snowy climate, you may need to either provide extra support within the greenhouse or be ready to remove snow whenever there is a significant snowfall because the lightweight aluminum frame members can easily bend under a heavy load. Before buying a kit, make sure to check on how snowfall may affect it.

Kit greenhouses are offered by many different manufacturers, and the exact assembly technique you use will depend on the specifics of your kit. Make sure you read the printed instructions carefully, as they may vary from this project.

The kit we're demonstrating here is made from aluminum frame pieces and transparent polycarbonate panels and is designed to be installed over a subbase of gravel about 5 inches thick. Other kits may have different subbase requirements.

When you purchase your kit, make sure to uncrate it and examine all the parts before you begin. Make sure all the pieces are there and that there are no damaged panels or bent frame members.

A perfectly flat and level base is crucial to any kit greenhouse, so make sure to work carefully. Try to do the work on a dry day with no wind, as the panels and frame pieces can be hard to manage on a windy day. Never try to build a kit greenhouse by yourself. At least one helper is mandatory, and you'll do even better with two or three.

Construction of a kit greenhouse consists of four basic steps: laying the base, assembling the frame, assembling the windows and doors, and attaching the panels.

Kit greenhouses come in a wide range of shapes, sizes, and quality. The best ones have tempered-glass glazing and are rather expensive. The one at right is glazed with corrugated polyethylene and is at the low end of the cost spectrum.

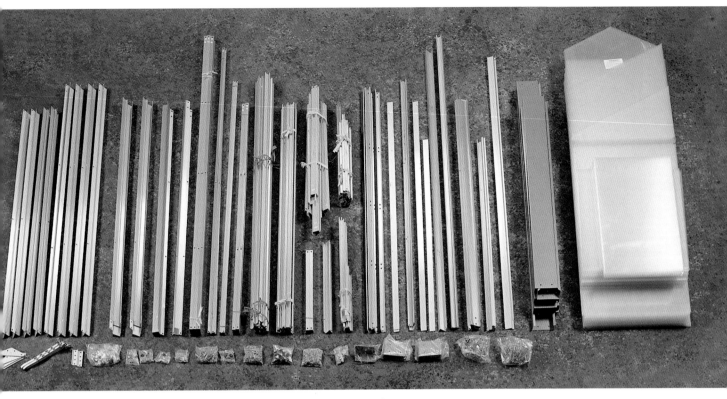

Organize and inspect the contents of your kit cartons to make sure all of the parts are present and in good condition. Most manuals will have a checklist. Staging the parts makes for a more efficient assembly. Just be sure not to leave any small parts loose, and do not store parts in high-traffic areas.

A cordless drill/driver with a nut-driver accessory will trim hours off of your assembly time compared with using only hand tools.

Rent outdoor power equipment if you need to do significant regrading to create a flat, level building base. Be sure to have your local utility company inspect for any buried utility lines first. (You may prefer to hire a landscaping company to do regrading work for you.)

How to Build a Freestanding Kit Greenhouse

Establish layout lines for the gravel subbase, using stakes or batterboards and mason's string. The excavation area for the subbase should be at least 2" wider and longer than the outside dimensions of the greenhouse kit base. Make sure the layout is perfectly square (the lines are perpendicular to one another) by measuring diagonally between opposing corners: the layout is square when the measurements are equal.

Excavate the site to a depth of 5", using the layout strings as a guide. As you work, use a straight 2 × 4 and a 4' level to check the excavation to make sure it is level and flat. Tamp any loose soil with a plate compactor or hand tamp. Cover the excavation with commercial-grade landscape fabric (do not use plastic; the membrane must be water-permeable). Fill the area with 2 or 3" of compactible gravel, grade and level it, then tamp it thoroughly. Add more gravel, level, and tamp for a final subbase depth of 5".

Assemble the greenhouse base, using the provided corner and end connectors. Set the base onto the subbase and make sure the base is level. Measure the diagonals to check for square, as before. Add a top dressing of gravel or other fill material inside the base, up to about 1" below the base's top lip. Smooth and level the gravel as before.

Attach the bottom wall plates to the base pieces so that the flanged edges face outside the greenhouse. In most systems, the floor plates will interlock with one another, end to end, with built-in brackets.

Fasten the four corner studs to the bottom wall plates, using hold-down connectors and bolts. In this system, each corner stud is secured with two connectors.

Install the ceiling plates: Assemble the pieces for each side ceiling plate. Attach each side plate against the inside of the two corner studs along each side of the greenhouse, making sure the gutter is positioned correctly. Attach the front ceiling plate to the outsides of the corner studs at the front of the building. *(continued)*

Attach the other side ceiling plate along the other side, flat against the inside of the corner studs. Then attach corner brackets to the rear studs, and construct the back top plate by attaching the rear braces to the corners and joining the braces together with stud connectors.

Corner bracket

Stud connectors

Fasten the left and right rear studs to the outside of the rear floor plate, making sure the top ends are sloping upward, toward the peak of the greenhouse. Attach the center rear studs to the rear floor plate, fastening them to the stud connectors used to join the rear braces.

BACKWARD AND FORWARD

With some kits you need to go backward to go forward. Because the individual parts of your kit depend upon one another for support, you may be required to tack all the parts together with bolts first and then undo and remake individual connections as you go before you can finalize them. For example, in this kit you must undo the track/brace connections one at a time so you can insert the bolt heads for the stud connectors into the track.

Install the doorway studs at either side of the greenhouse door on the front end of the building. Install the side studs along both side walls of the greenhouse.

Add diagonal struts, as directed by the manufacturer. The struts help to stiffen and square up the walls. As you work, take diagonal measurements between opposing corners at the tops of the walls, to make sure the structure remains square.

Fasten the gable-end stud extensions to the front and back walls of the greenhouse. The top ends of the studs should angle upward, toward the peak of the greenhouse.

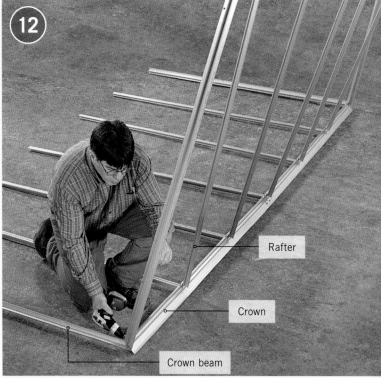

Assemble the roof frame on a flat area near the wall assembly. First assemble the crown-beam pieces; then attach the rafters to the crown, one by one. The end rafters, called the crown beams, have a different configuration, so make sure not to confuse them. *(continued)*

With at least one helper, lift the roof into place onto the wall frames. The gable end studs should meet the outside edges of the crown beams, and the ends of the crown beams rest on the outer edge of the corner bracket. Fasten in place with the provided nuts and bolts.

Attach the side braces and the roof-window support beams to the underside of the roof rafters, as specified by the manufacturer's instructions.

Build the roof windows by first connecting the two side window frames to the top window frame. Slide the window panel into the frame; then secure it by attaching the bottom window frame. Slide the window into the slot at the top of the roof crown; then gradually lower it in place. Attach the window stop to the window support beam.

Assemble the doors, making sure the top slider/roller bar and the bottom slider bar are correctly positioned. Lift the door panels up into place onto the top and bottom wall plates.

Install the panels one by one, using panel clips. Begin with the large wall panels. Position each panel and secure it by snapping a clip into the frame, at the intervals specified by the manufacturer's instructions.

Add the upper panels. At the gable ends, the upper panels will be supported by panel connectors that allow the top panel to be supported by the bottom panel. The lower panels should be installed already.

Install the roof panels and roof-window panels so that the top edges fit up under the edge of the crown or window support and the bottom edges align over the gutters.

Test the door and window operation, and make any necessary adjustments so they open and close smoothly.

PVC Hoophouse

The hoophouse is a popular garden structure for two main reasons: it is cheap to build and easy to build. In many agricultural areas you will see hoophouses snaking across vast fields of seedlings, protecting the delicate plants at their most vulnerable stages. Because they are portable and easy to disassemble, they can be removed when the plants are established and less vulnerable.

While hoophouses are not intended as inexpensive substitutes for real greenhouses, they do serve an important agricultural purpose. And building your own is a fun project that the whole family can enjoy.

The hoophouse shown here is essentially a Quonset-style frame of bent ¾-inch PVC tubing draped with sheet plastic. Each semicircular frame is actually made from two 10-foot lengths of tubing that fit into a plastic fitting at the apex of the curve. PVC tubes tend to stay together simply by friction-fitting into the fittings, so you don't normally need to solvent glue the connections (this is important to the easy-to-disassemble and store feature). If you experience problems with the frame connections separating, try cutting 4- to 6-inch-long pieces of ½-inch (outside diameter) PVC tubing and inserting them into the tubes and fittings like splines. This will stiffen the connections.

A hoophouse is a temporary agricultural structure designed to be low-cost and portable. Also called Quonset houses and tunnel houses, hoophouses provide shelter and shade (depending on the film you use) and protection from wind and the elements. They will boost heat during the day, but are less efficient than paneled greenhouses for extending the growing season.

PVC HOOPHOUSE

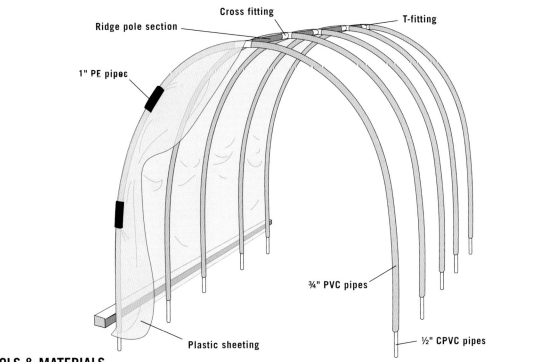

Cross fitting

Ridge pole section

T-fitting

1" PE pipe

¾" PVC pipes

½" CPVC pipes

Plastic sheeting

TOOLS & MATERIALS

Hand sledge

Plastic tubing cutter or hacksaw

Wood or rubber mallet

Circular saw

Stapler

Drill

Utility knife

Stakes and mason's string

Eye and ear protection

Tape measure

Work gloves

(5) ½" × 10' CPVC pipes

(14) ¾" × 10' PVC pipes

(3) ¾" PVC cross fittings

(2) ¾" PVC T-fittings

16 × 24' clear or translucent plastic sheeting

(4) 16' pressure-treated 2 × 4s

2½" deck screws

(1) 1" × 6' PE tubing (black, flexible)

BUILDING A HOOPHOUSE

- Space frame hoops about 3' apart.

- Leave ridge members a fraction of an inch (not more than ¼") shorter than the span, which will cause the structure to be slightly shorter on top than at the base. This helps stabilize the structure.

- Orient the structure so the wall faces into the prevailing wind rather than the end openings.

- If you are using long-lasting greenhouse fabric for the cover, protect the investment by spray-painting the frame hoops with primer so there is no plastic-to-plastic contact.

- Because hoophouses are temporary structures that are designed to be disassembled or moved regularly, you do not need to include a base.

- Hoophouses can act a lot like boat sails and will fly away if they're not anchored securely. Be sure to stake each hoop to the ground at both ends (with 30" or longer stakes), and carefully weight down the cover with boards (as shown here) or piles of dirt.

- Clip the hoophouse covers to the end frames. Clips fastened at the intermediate hoops will either fly off or tear the plastic cover in windy conditions.

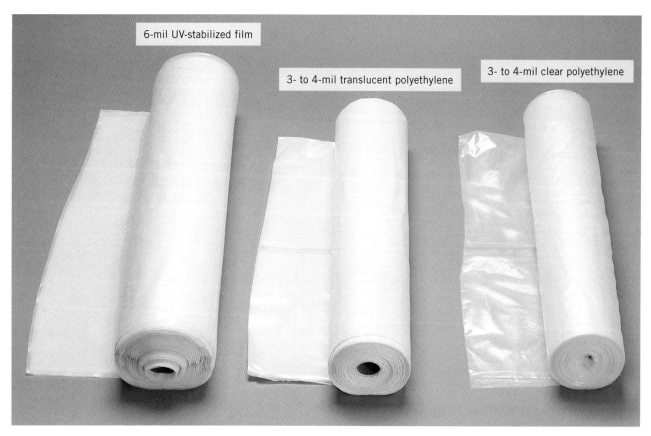

6-mil UV-stabilized film

3- to 4-mil translucent polyethylene

3- to 4-mil clear polyethylene

Sheet plastic is an inexpensive material for creating a greenhouse. Obviously, it is less durable than polycarbonate, fiberglass or glass panels. But UV-stabilized films at least 6-mil thick can be rated to withstand four years or more of exposure. Inexpensive polyethylene sheeting (the kind you find at hardware stores) will hold up for a year or two, but it becomes brittle when exposed to sunlight. Some greenhouse builders prefer to use clear plastic sheeting to maximize the sunlight penetration, but the cloudiness of translucent poly makes it effective for diffusing light and preventing overheating. For the highest quality film coverings, look for film rated for greenhouse and agricultural use.

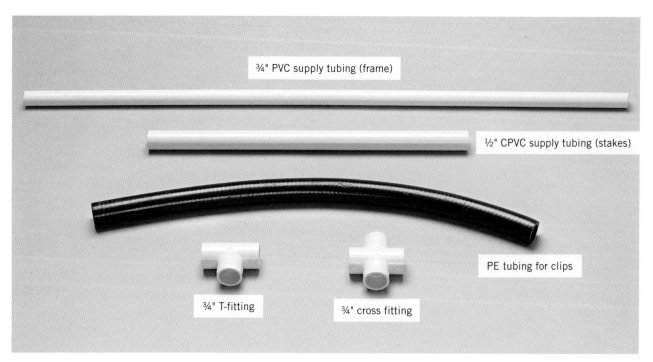

¾" PVC supply tubing (frame)

½" CPVC supply tubing (stakes)

PE tubing for clips

¾" T-fitting

¾" cross fitting

Plastic tubing and fittings used to build this hoophouse include: light-duty ¾" PVC tubing for the frame (do not use CPVC—it is too rigid and won't bend properly); ½" CPVC supply tubing for the frame stakes (rigidity is good here); polyethylene (PE) tubing for the cover clips; T-fittings and cross fittings to join the frame members.

How to Build a PVC Hoophouse

Lay out the installation area, using stakes and mason's string. Stake the four corners to create a rectangle that is 10' wide and 15' long. To make sure the layout is square (the strings are perpendicular), measure diagonally between opposing corner stakes: when the measurements are equal, the layout is square.

Cut a 30"-long stake from ½" CPVC pipe for each leg of each frame hoop. Plastic pipe is easy to cut with a plastic tubing cutter or a hacksaw. Mark the layout strings at 36" intervals, using tape or a marker. Drive a stake at each marked location, using a hand sledge or hammer. Keep the stakes plumb and drive them in 20" deep, so only 10" is above ground.

Join the two legs for each frame hoop with a fitting. Use a T-fitting for the end hoop frames and a cross fitting for the intermediate hoop frames. No priming or solvent gluing is necessary. (The friction-fit should be sufficient, but it helps if you tap on the end of the fitting with a mallet to seat it.)

(continued)

Slip the open end of one hoop-frame leg over a corner stake so the pipe is flush against the ground. Then bend the pipes so you can fit the other leg end over the stake at the opposite corner. If you experience problems with the pipes pulling out of the top fitting, simply tape the joints temporarily until the structure frame is completed.

Continue adding hoop frames until you reach the other end of the structure. Wait until all the hoop frames are in place before you begin installing the ridge poles. Make sure the cross fittings on the intermediate hoop frames are aligned correctly to accept the ridge poles.

Add the ridge pole sections to tie together the hoop frames. The correct length for the ridge poles depends on the socket depth of the fitting you use, so you'll have to measure the fittings and calculate length of the ridge pieces. If necessary, tap the end of each ridge piece with a wood or rubber mallet to seat it fully in the fitting socket.

Cut four 2 × 4s to length (15' as shown). Cut the cover material to length at 16' (or as needed so it is several inches longer than the house at both ends). Staple one edge of the cover to one of the 2 × 4s, keeping the material taut and flat as you work from one end to the other

Lay another 2 × 4 over the first so their ends and edges are flush and the cover material is sandwiched in between. Fasten the two boards together with 2½" deck screws driven every 24" or so. Position the board assembly along the base of the hoops and pull the free end of the material over the tops of the hoops to the other side.

Pull the cover taut on the other side of the house, and repeat the process of stapling it to one board then sandwiching with the other.

Secure the cover at the ends with 6" lengths of 1" PE tubing. Cut the tubing pieces to length, then slit them lengthwise to create simple clips. Use at least six clips at each end of the house. Do not use clips on the intermediate hoops.

OPTION: Make doors by clipping a piece of cover material to each end. (It's best to do this before attaching the main cover.) Then cut a slit down the center of the end material. You can tie or tape the door material to the sides when you want it open and weigh down the pieces with a board or brick to keep the door shut. This solution is low-tech but effective.

Shed-Style Greenhouse

TOOLS & MATERIALS

Circular saw	Framing square
Power miter saw	Plumb bob
Hammer	Caulk
Level	Caulk gun
Hand tamper	Screwdriver
Ladder	Work gloves
Eye & ear protection	

This unique outbuilding is part greenhouse and part shed, making it perfect for a year-round garden space or backyard sunroom, or even an artist's studio. The front facade is dominated by windows—four 29- × 72-inch windows on the roof, plus four 29- × 18-inch windows on the front wall. When appointed as a greenhouse, two long planting tables inside the shed let you water and tend to plants without flooding the floor. If gardening isn't in your plans, you can omit the tables and cover the entire floor with plywood, or perhaps fill in between the floor timbers with pavers or stones.

Some other details that make this 10- × 12-foot shed stand out are the homemade Dutch door, with top and bottom halves that you can open together or independently, and its traditional saltbox shape. The roof covering shown here consists of standard asphalt shingles, but cedar shingles make for a nice upgrade.

Because sunlight plays a central role in this shed design, consider the location and orientation carefully. To avoid shadows from nearby structures, maintain a distance between the shed and the structure that's at least 2½ times the height of the obstruction. With all of that sunlight, the temperature inside the shed is another important consideration. You may want to install some roof vents to release hot air and water vapor.

Building the Shed-Style Greenhouse involves a few unconventional construction steps. First, the side walls are framed in two parts: You build the square portion of the endwalls first, then move onto the roof framing. After the rafters are up, you complete the "rake," or angled, sections of the side walls. This makes it easy to measure for each wall stud, rather than having to calculate the lengths beforehand. Second, the shed's 4 × 4 floor structure also serves as its foundation. The plywood floor decking goes on after the walls are installed, rather than before.

With slight modifications, many ordinary sheds can be redesigned as greenhouses. The addition of glass roof panels turns this shed design into an effective greenhouse.

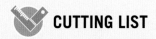

CUTTING LIST

PART	QUANTITY/SIZE	MATERIAL
Foundation/Floor		
Foundation base & interior drainage beds	5 cu. yds.	Compactible gravel
Floor joists & blocking	7 @ 10'	4 × 4 pressure-treated landscape timbers
4 × 4 blocking	1 @ 10' 1 @ 8'	4 × 4 pressure-treated landscape timbers
Box sills (rim joists)	2 @ 12'	2 × 4 pressure-treated
Nailing cleats & 2 × 4 blocking	2 @ 8'	2 × 4 pressure-treated
Floor sheathing	2 sheets @ 4 × 8'	¾" ext.-grade plywood
Wall Framing		
Bottom plates	2 @ 12', 2 @ 10'	2 × 4 pressure-treated
Top plates	4 @ 12', 2 @ 10'	2 × 4
Studs	43 @ 8'	2 × 4
Door header & jack studs	3 @ 8'	2 × 4
Rafter header	2 @ 12'	2 × 8
Roof Framing		
Rafters—A & C, & nailers	10 @ 12'	2 × 4
Rafters—B & lookouts	10 @ 10'	2 × 4
Ridge board	1 @ 14'	2 × 6
Exterior Finishes		
Rear fascia	1 @ 14'	1 × 6 cedar
Rear soffit	1 @ 14'	1 × 8 cedar
Gable fascia (rake board) & soffit	4 @ 16'	1 × 6 cedar
Siding	10 sheets @ 4 × 8'	⅝" Texture 1-11 plywood siding
Siding flashing	10 linear ft.	Metal Z-flashing
Trim*	4 @ 12'	1 × 4 cedar
	1 @ 12'	1 × 2 cedar
Wall corner trim	6 @ 8'	1 × 4 cedar
Roofing		
Sheathing	5 sheets @ 4 × 8'	½" exterior-grade plywood roof sheathing
15# building paper	1 roll	
Drip edge	72 linear ft.	Metal drip edge
Shingles	2⅔ squares	Asphalt shingles—250# per sq. min.

PART	QUANTITY/SIZE	MATERIAL
Windows		
Glazing	4 pieces @ 31¼ × 76½" 4 pieces @ 31¼ × 20¾"	¼"-thick clear plastic glazing
Window stops	12 @ 10'	2 × 4
Glazing tape	60 linear ft.	
Clear exterior caulk	5 tubes	
Door		
Trim & stops	3 @ 8'	1 × 2 cedar
Surround	4 @ 8'	2 × 2 cedar
Z-flashing	3 linear ft.	
Plant Tables (Optional)		
Front table, top & trim	6 @ 12'	1 × 6 cedar or pressure-treated
Front table, plates & legs	4 @ 12'	2 × 4 pressure-treated
Rear table, top & trim	6 @ 8'	1 × 6 cedar or pressure-treated
Rear table, plates & legs	4 @ 8'	2 × 4 pressure-treated
Fasteners & Hardware		
16d galvanized common nails	5 lbs.	
16d common nails	16 lbs.	
10d common nails	1½ lbs.	
8d galvanized common nails	2 lbs.	
8d galvanized box nails	3 lbs.	
10d galvanized finish nails	2½ lbs.	
8d galvanized siding nails	8 lbs.	
1" galvanized roofing nails	7 lbs.	
8d galvanized casing nails	3 lbs.	
6d galvanized casing nails	2 lbs.	
Door hinges with screws	4 @ 3½"	Corrosion-resistant hinges
Door handle	1	
Sliding bolt latch	1	
Construction adhesive	1 tube	

Note: The 1 × 4 trim bevel at the bottom of the sloped windows can be steeper (45° or more) so the trim slopes away from the window if there is concern that the trim may capture water running down the glazing (see WINDOW DETAIL, page 116).

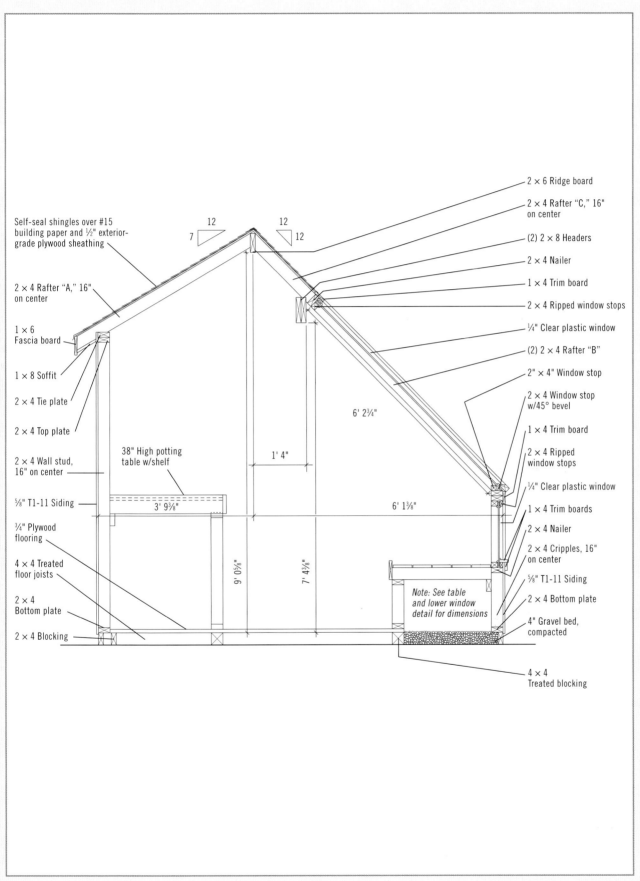

Self-seal shingles over #15 building paper and ½" exterior-grade plywood sheathing

2 × 4 Rafter "A," 16" on center

1 × 6 Fascia board

1 × 8 Soffit

2 × 4 Tie plate

2 × 4 Top plate

2 × 4 Wall stud, 16" on center

⅝" T1-11 Siding

¾" Plywood flooring

4 × 4 Treated floor joists

2 × 4 Bottom plate

2 × 4 Blocking

38" High potting table w/shelf

3' 9⅜"

9' 0⅝"

7' 4⅜"

1' 4"

6' 2¾"

6' 1⅜"

Note: See table and lower window detail for dimensions

12
7

12
12

2 × 6 Ridge board

2 × 4 Rafter "C," 16" on center

(2) 2 × 8 Headers

2 × 4 Nailer

1 × 4 Trim board

2 × 4 Ripped window stops

¼" Clear plastic window

(2) 2 × 4 Rafter "B"

2" × 4" Window stop

2 × 4 Window stop w/45° bevel

1 × 4 Trim board

2 × 4 Ripped window stops

¼" Clear plastic window

1 × 4 Trim boards

2 × 4 Nailer

2 × 4 Cripples, 16" on center

⅝" T1-11 Siding

2 × 4 Bottom plate

4" Gravel bed, compacted

4 × 4 Treated blocking

FLOOR FRAMING PLAN

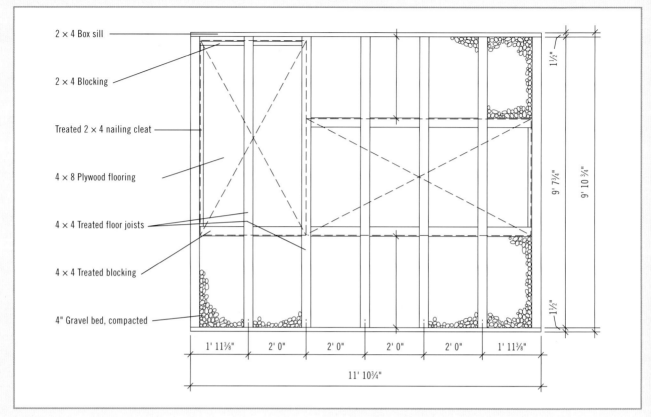

2 × 4 Box sill

2 × 4 Blocking

Treated 2 × 4 nailing cleat

4 × 8 Plywood flooring

4 × 4 Treated floor joists

4 × 4 Treated blocking

4" Gravel bed, compacted

1½"

9' 7¾" 9' 10¾"

1½"

1' 11⅜" · 2' 0" · 2' 0" · 2' 0" · 2' 0" · 1' 11⅜"

11' 10¾"

LEFT SIDE FRAMING

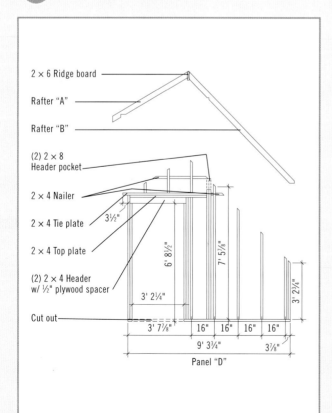

2 × 6 Ridge board

Rafter "A"

Rafter "B"

(2) 2 × 8 Header pocket

2 × 4 Nailer

3½"

2 × 4 Tie plate

2 × 4 Top plate

(2) 2 × 4 Header w/ ½" plywood spacer

Cut out

6' 8½"   7' 5⅝"

3' 2¼"

3' 2¾"

3' 7⅞" · 16" · 16" · 16" · 16"

9' 3¾"   3⅞"

Panel "D"

RIGHT SIDE FRAMING

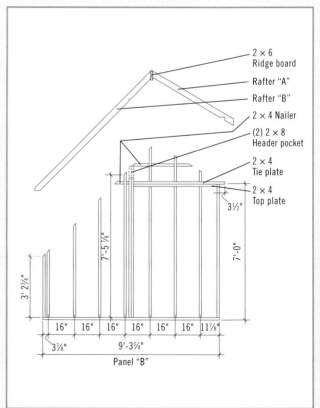

2 × 6 Ridge board

Rafter "A"

Rafter "B"

2 × 4 Nailer

(2) 2 × 8 Header pocket

2 × 4 Tie plate

3½"

2 × 4 Top plate

3' 2¾"

7'-5⅝"

7'-0"

16" · 16" · 16" · 16" · 16" · 16" · 11⅞"

3⅞"   9'-3¾"

Panel "B"

🔨 FRONT FRAMING

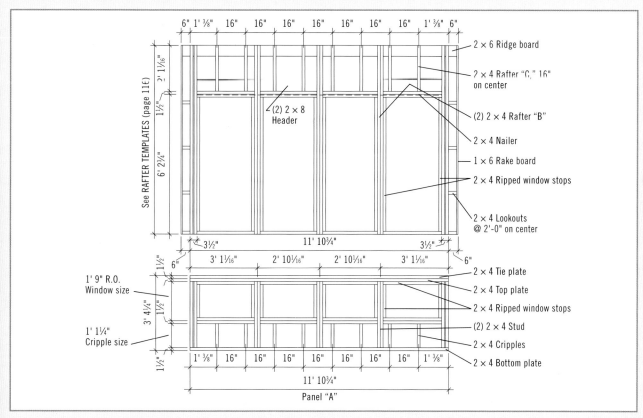

6" 1' ⅜" 16" 16" 16" 16" 16" 16" 16" 1' ⅜" 6"

See RAFTER TEMPLATES (page 116)

2' 1¹¹⁄₁₆"
1½"
6' 2¾"

2 × 6 Ridge board

2 × 4 Rafter "C," 16" on center

(2) 2 × 8 Header

(2) 2 × 4 Rafter "B"

2 × 4 Nailer

1 × 6 Rake board

2 × 4 Ripped window stops

2 × 4 Lookouts @ 2'-0" on center

3½"   11' 10¾"   3½"

6"   3' 1¹⁄₁₆"   2' 10¹⁄₁₆"   2' 10¹⁄₁₆"   3' 1¹⁄₁₆"   6"

1½"

1' 9" R.O. Window size

3' 4¼"
1½"

1' 1¼" Cripple size

1½"

2 × 4 Tie plate
2 × 4 Top plate
2 × 4 Ripped window stops
(2) 2 × 4 Stud
2 × 4 Cripples
2 × 4 Bottom plate

1' ⅜" 16" 16" 16" 16" 16" 16" 16" 1' ⅜"

11' 10¾"

Panel "A"

🔨 REAR FRAMING

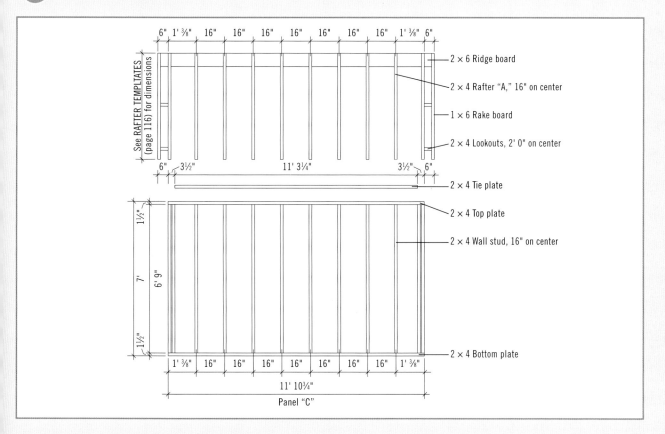

6" 1' ⅜" 16" 16" 16" 16" 16" 16" 16" 1' ⅜" 6"

See RAFTER TEMPLTAES (page 116) for dimensions

2 × 6 Ridge board

2 × 4 Rafter "A," 16" on center

1 × 6 Rake board

2 × 4 Lookouts, 2' 0" on center

6"   3½"   11' 3¼"   3½"   6"

2 × 4 Tie plate

2 × 4 Top plate

1½"

7'   6' 9"

2 × 4 Wall stud, 16" on center

1½"

2 × 4 Bottom plate

1' ⅜" 16" 16" 16" 16" 16" 16" 16" 1' ⅜"

11' 10¾"

Panel "C"

FRONT ELEVATION

REAR ELEVATION

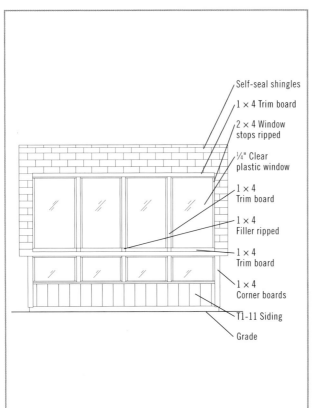

Self-seal shingles

1 × 4 Trim board

2 × 4 Window stops ripped

¼" Clear plastic window

1 × 4 Trim board

1 × 4 Filler ripped

1 × 4 Trim board

1 × 4 Corner boards

T1-11 Siding

Grade

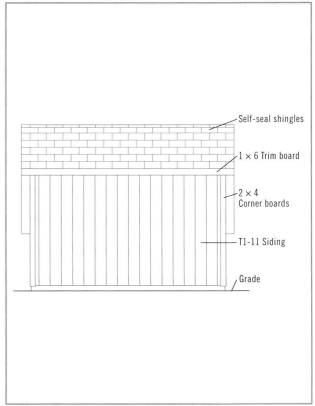

Self-seal shingles

1 × 6 Trim board

2 × 4 Corner boards

T1-11 Siding

Grade

RIGHT SIDE ELEVATION

SOFFIT DETAIL

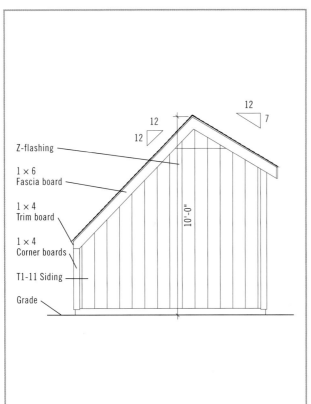

Z-flashing

1 × 6 Fascia board

1 × 4 Trim board

1 × 4 Corner boards

T1-11 Siding

Grade

12
12
12
7

10'-0"

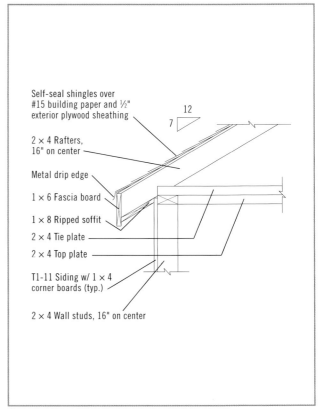

Self-seal shingles over #15 building paper and ½" exterior plywood sheathing

2 × 4 Rafters, 16" on center

Metal drip edge

1 × 6 Fascia board

1 × 8 Ripped soffit

2 × 4 Tie plate

2 × 4 Top plate

T1-11 Siding w/ 1 × 4 corner boards (typ.)

2 × 4 Wall studs, 16" on center

12
7

FRONT & SIDE DOOR CONSTRUCTION

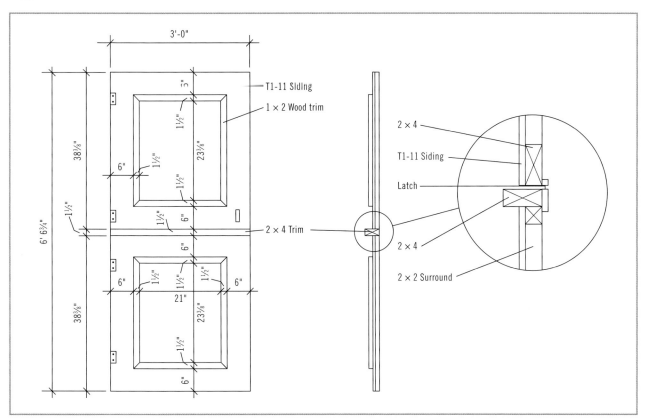

FRONT & SIDE DOOR CONSTRUCTION (DOORJAMB, REAR, DOOR HEADER)

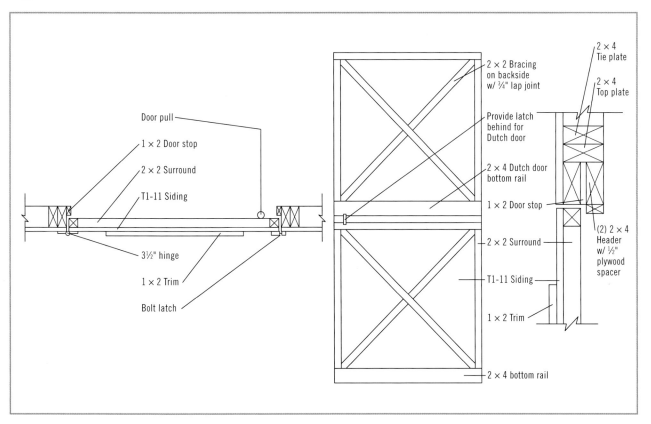

HEADER & WINDOW DETAIL

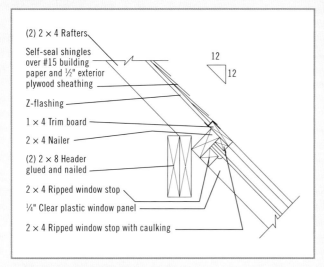

(2) 2 × 4 Rafters

Self-seal shingles over #15 building paper and ½" exterior plywood sheathing

Z-flashing

1 × 4 Trim board

2 × 4 Nailer

(2) 2 × 8 Header glued and nailed

2 × 4 Ripped window stop

¼" Clear plastic window panel

2 × 4 Ripped window stop with caulking

12
12

WINDOW SECTION

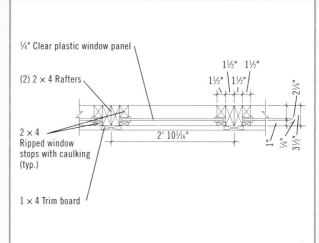

¼" Clear plastic window panel

(2) 2 × 4 Rafters

2 × 4 Ripped window stops with caulking (typ.)

1 × 4 Trim board

1½" 1½"
1½" 1½"
2¼"
2' 10¹⁄₁₆"
1" ¼" 3½"

WINDOW DETAIL

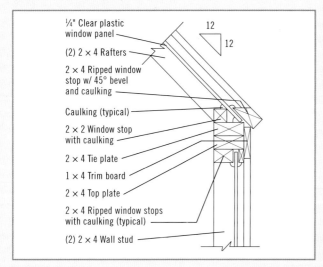

¼" Clear plastic window panel

(2) 2 × 4 Rafters

2 × 4 Ripped window stop w/ 45° bevel and caulking

Caulking (typical)

2 × 2 Window stop with caulking

2 × 4 Tie plate

1 × 4 Trim board

2 × 4 Top plate

2 × 4 Ripped window stops with caulking (typical)

(2) 2 × 4 Wall stud

12
12

TABLE & LOWER WINDOW DETAIL

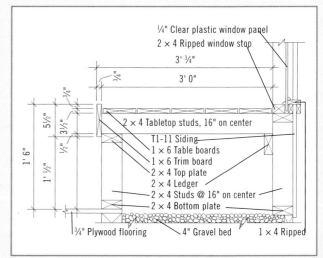

¼" Clear plastic window panel

2 × 4 Ripped window stop

3' ¾"
3' 0"
¾"
¾"

2 × 4 Tabletop studs, 16" on center

T1-11 Siding
1 × 6 Table boards
1 × 6 Trim board
2 × 4 Top plate
2 × 4 Ledger
2 × 4 Studs @ 16" on center
2 × 4 Bottom plate

1' 6"
1' 1½"
5½"
3½"
½"
1½"

¾" Plywood flooring   4" Gravel bed   1 × 4 Ripped

RAFTER TEMPLATES

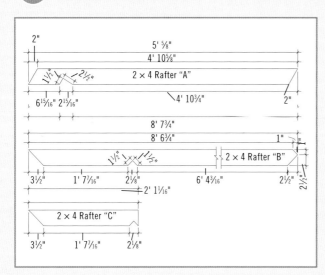

2"
5' ⁵⁄₈"
4' 10⁵⁄₈"
2 × 4 Rafter "A"
4' 10¾"
1½" 2½"
6¹⁵⁄₁₆" 2⁵⁄₁₆"
2"

8' 7¾"
8' 6¾"
1"
2 × 4 Rafter "B"
1½" 1½"
3½" 1' 7⁷⁄₁₆" 2⅛" 6' 4³⁄₁₆" 2½"
2½"
2' 1¹⁄₁₆"

2 × 4 Rafter "C"
3½" 1' 7⁷⁄₁₆" 2⅛"

RAKE BOARD DETAIL

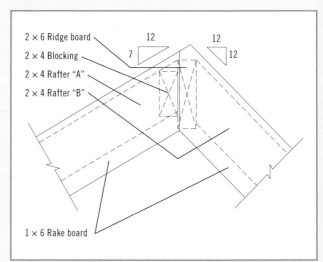

2 × 6 Ridge board
2 × 4 Blocking
2 × 4 Rafter "A"
2 × 4 Rafter "B"

12
12
7

1 × 6 Rake board

How to Build a Shed-Style Greenhouse

Build the foundation, following the basic steps used for a wooden skid foundation. First, prepare a bed of compacted gravel. Make sure the bed is flat and level. Cut seven 4 × 4" × 10' pressure-treated posts down to 115¾" to serve as floor joists. Position the joists as shown in the FLOOR FRAMING PLAN. Level each joist, and make sure all are level with one another and the ends are flush. Add rim joists and blocking: Cut two 12' 2 × 4s (142¾") for rim joists. Fasten the rim joists to the ends of the 4 × 4 joists (see the FLOOR FRAMING PLAN) with 16d galvanized common nails.

Cut ten 4 × 4 blocks to fit between the joists. Install six blocks 34½" from the front rim joist, and install four blocks 31½" from the rear. Toenail the blocks to the joists. All blocks, joists, and sills must be flush at the top.

To frame the rear wall, cut one top plate and one pressure-treated bottom plate (142¾"). Cut twelve studs (81"). Assemble the wall following the layout in the REAR FRAMING (page 113). Raise the wall and fasten it to the rear rim joist and the intermediate joists, using 16d galvanized common nails. Brace the wall in position with 2 × 4 braces staked to the ground.

For the front wall, cut two top plates and one treated bottom plate (142¾"). Cut ten studs (35¾") and eight cripple studs (13¼"). Cut four 2 × 4 window sills (311⁄16"). Assemble the wall following the layout in the FRONT FRAMING (page 113). Add the double top plate, but do not install the window stops at this time. Raise, attach, and brace the front wall.

(continued)

Cut lumber for the right side wall: one top plate (54⅞"), one treated bottom plate (111¾"), four studs (81"), and two header post studs (86⅞"); and for the left side wall: top plate (54⅞"), bottom plate (111¾"), three studs (81"), two jack studs (77½"), two posts (86⅞"), and a built-up 2 × 4 header (39¼"). Assemble and install the walls as shown in the RIGHT SIDE FRAMING and LEFT SIDE FRAMING (page 112). Add the doubled top plates along the rear and side walls. Install treated 2 × 4 nailing cleats to the joists and blocking as shown in the FLOOR FRAMING PLAN (page 112) and BUILDING SECTION (page 111).

Trim two sheets of ¾" plywood as needed and install them over the joists and blocking as shown in the FLOOR FRAMING PLAN, leaving open cavities along the front of the shed and a portion of the rear. Fasten the sheets with 8d galvanized common nails driven every 6" along the edges and 8" in the field. Fill the exposed foundation cavities with 4" of gravel and compact it thoroughly.

Construct the rafter header from two 2 × 8s cut to 142¾". Join the pieces with construction adhesive and pairs of 10d common nails driven every 24" on both sides. Set the header on top of the side wall posts, and toenail it to the posts with four 16d common nails at each end.

Cut one of each "A" and "B" pattern rafters using the RAFTER TEMPLATES (page 116). Test-fit the rafters. The B rafter should rest squarely on the rafter header, and its bottom end should sit flush with outside of the front wall. Adjust the rafter cuts as needed, then use the pattern rafters to mark and cut the remaining A and B rafters.

Cut the 2 × 6 ridge board (154¾"). Mark the rafter layout onto the ridge and front and rear wall plates following the FRONT FRAMING and REAR FRAMING. Install the A and B rafters and ridge. Make sure the B rafters are spaced accurately so the windows will fit properly into their frames; see the WINDOW SECTION (page 116).

Cut a pattern "C" rafter, test-fit, and adjust as needed. Cut the remaining seven C rafters and install them. Measure and cut four 2 × 4 nailers (311⅛6") to fit between the sets of B rafters (as shown). Position the nailers as shown in the HEADER & WINDOW DETAIL (page 116) and toenail them to the rafters.

Complete the rake portions of each side wall. Mark the stud layouts onto the bottom plate, and onto the top plate of the square wall section; see the RIGHT and LEFT SIDE FRAMING. Use a plumb bob to transfer the layout to the rafters. Measure for each stud, cutting the top ends of the studs under the B rafters at 45° and those under the A rafters at 30°. Toenail the studs to the plates and rafters. Add horizontal 2 × 4 nailers as shown in the framing drawings.

Create the inner and outer window stops from 10'-long 2 × 4s. For stops at the sides and tops of the roof windows and all sides of the front wall windows, rip the inner stops to 2¼" wide and the outer stops to 1" wide; see the WINDOW SECTION and WINDOW DETAIL (page 116). For the bottom of each roof window, rip the inner stop to 1½"; bevel the edge of the outer stop at 45°.

(continued)

Install each window as follows. Attach inner stops as shown in the drawings, using galvanized finish nails. Paint or varnish the rafters and stops for moisture protection. Apply a heavy bead of caulk at each location shown on the drawings (HEADER & WINDOW DETAIL, WINDOW SECTION/DETAIL, TABLE & LOWER WINDOW DETAIL). Set the glazing in place, add another bead of caulk, and attach the outer stops. Cover the rafters and stop edges with 1 × 4 trim.

Cover the walls with T1-11 siding, starting with the rear wall. Trim the sheets as needed so they extend from the bottom edges of the rafters down to at least 1" below the tops of the foundation timbers. On the side walls, add Z-flashing above the first row and continue the siding up to the rafters.

Install 1 × 6 fascia over the ends of the A rafters. Keep all fascia ½" above the rafters so it will be flush with the roof sheathing. Using scrap rafter material, cut the 2 × 4 lookouts (5¼"). On each outer B rafter, install one lookout at the bottom end and four more spaced 24" on center going up. On the A rafters, add a lookout at both ends and two spaced evenly in between. Install the 1 × 6 rake boards (fascia) as shown in the RAKE BOARD DETAIL (page 116).

Soffit

Rip 1 × 6 boards to 5¼" width (some may come milled to 5¼" already) for the gable soffits. Fasten the soffits to the lookouts with siding nails. Rip a 1 × 8 board for the soffit along the rear eave, beveling the edges at 30° to match the A rafter ends. Install the soffit.

Deck the roof with ½" plywood sheathing, starting at the bottom ends of the rafters. Install metal drip edge, building paper, and asphalt shingles. If desired, add one or more roof vents during the shingle installation. Be sure to overlap shingles onto the 1 × 4 trim board above the roof windows, as shown in the HEADER & WINDOW DETAIL.

Construct the planting tables from 2 × 4 lumber and 1 × 6 boards, as shown in the TABLE & LOWER WINDOW DETAIL and BUILDING SECTION. The bottom plates of the table legs should be flush with the outside edges of foundation blocking.

Build each of the two door panels using T1-11 siding, 2 × 2 bracing, a 2 × 4 bottom rail, and 1 × 2 trim on the front side; see the DOOR CONSTRUCTION drawings (page 115). The panels are identical except for a 2 × 4 sill added to the top of the lower panel. Install 1 × 2 stops at the sides and top of the door opening. Hang the doors with four hinges, leaving even gaps all around. Install a bolt latch for locking the two panels together.

Complete the trim details with 1 × 4 vertical corner boards, 1 × 4 horizontal trim above the front wall windows, and ripped 1 × 4 trim and 1 × 2 trim at the bottom of the front wall windows (see the TABLE & LOWER WINDOW DETAIL). Paint the siding and trim, or coat with exterior wood finish.

Sun Porch Kit

A sun porch, a sunroom, a three-season porch, a greenhouse, a hothouse, an orangerie, a conservatory . . . these names are not precisely interchangeable, but all refer to a similar type of room. The common element all types share is that their walls and usually their roofs are made of clear panel glazing that allows light in and traps it, raising the ambient room temperature to more comfortable levels in cooler times of year. Some of these structures are designed for gardening-related activities; others are meant for enjoyment or entertainment. Some are freestanding, others are attached to a house.

If it is custom-built for you by a professional contractor, a sunroom can be quite expensive. But there is another option: a sunroom in a box. You can have a complete, do-it-yourself sunroom kit delivered to your home in cardboard boxes. A good deal of assembly is required, of course, but with a few basic tools and a helper, most people with basic DIY skills can complete the job in a weekend.

The key features of this sun porch (manufactured by SunPorch Structures Inc., see Resources page 236)

are its easy installation and its versatility. First, it's designed to install right on top of an existing concrete patio slab or a wood deck, eliminating the extensive site-prep work required with a custom project. If you don't have a patio or deck in place, you can build an inexpensive foundation with landscape timbers to support the sunroom structure, then create a floor inside using brick pavers, stone, wood decking tiles, or other suitable material. The sunroom manufacturer and your local building department can help you with the planning and construction details.

The sunroom's versatility is apparent in both its design and use. Its modular construction allows you to specify the height, width, and length of the structure to fit your needs and your house. Other modifications can be made at the factory to accommodate special installation requirements, such as installing the room to fit against the roof eave of your house or even slightly above the eave. The standard room design includes two matching endwalls and a front wall. If your sunroom will fit into a corner where two house walls meet, simply order the room without one of the endwalls. The sizes of endwalls also can be adjusted to fit other house configurations.

Operable and removable windows make this sunroom versatile to use. In cooler months, all the windows can be closed against the cold to keep the sun's heat inside. As the weather warms up, you can open either the top or bottom window sash to capture the breezes. And in the summer, you can take the windows out completely to convert the sunroom into a fully screened patio room.

CHECK IN WITH YOUR BUILDING DEPARTMENT

It's up to you to gain legal approval for your sunroom project. Contact your city's building department to learn what its rules are. Some municipalities require permits and inspections for DIY sunrooms, while others exclude structures that are installed over existing patios or decks and do not change the home's footprint. In any case, you should also consult with a qualified building professional to make sure your patio, deck, or other foundation can safely support a sunroom.

A DIY sunroom kit comes with all of the parts precut and predrilled for your own custom design. Assembling the kit is a relatively easy task that most couples can accomplish in a weekend.

Commercial-grade, lightweight glazing, and predrilled aluminum frame parts are the key components that make this sunroom kit lightweight and durable enough for shipping and also easy to assemble. Sunrooms can be perfectly acceptable spaces for evening activities, if you equip them with light fixtures (left).

Sun Porch Kit Accessories

Skylight shades give you control over light and heat coming through the roof panels. These 2-in-1 shades have a solid reflective panel that blocks most of the sun's light and heat and a translucent panel that blocks only half of the sunlight to reduce glare and heat gain while letting light filter through.

Precisely fitted wall shades are convenient for reducing glare and heat gain right where you need it. They're also great for adding privacy when and where you want it without blocking all of your sunroom views.

Optional roof vents allow hot air to escape and help to flush the interior of the sunroom with fresh air. Adjustable covers let you control the rate of airflow. The opening and closing mechanism is easy to operate from inside the sun porch.

Options for Attaching a Sun Porch to Your House

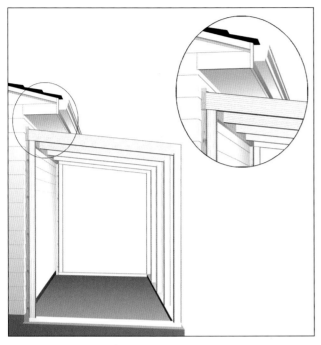

Attach the ledger directly to the wall if there is no eave overhang or if there is at least 6" of clear working space between the top of the ledger and the bottom of the eaves.

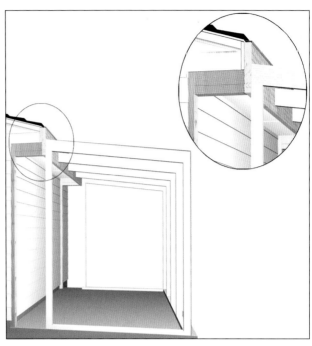

If the maximum height of the sun porch brings it up against or within 6" of the bottom of the eave overhang, extend the fascia on the eave downward and fill in with boards or siding between the cornice and the back post for the sun porch.

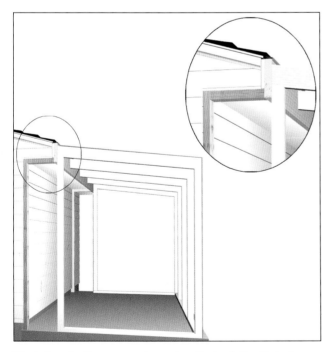

The ledger for the sun porch can be attached directly to the fascia board as long as the highest point of the sun-porch roof remains slightly lower than the roof covering. Be sure to attach the ledger so the lag screws hit into the ends of the rafter tails.

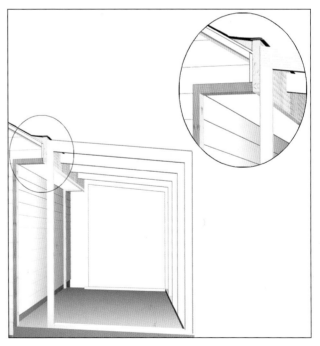

If the sun porch is slightly taller than the roof eaves, you can add a ledger that's taller than the fascia, but it cannot extend more than a couple of inches higher. Fill in the open area beneath the roof covering created at the side using a full-width wood wedge and caulk. The roof covering must retain a slight slope with no swales.

Preparing the Installation Site

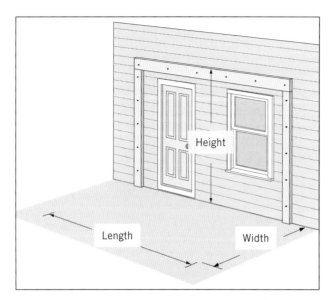

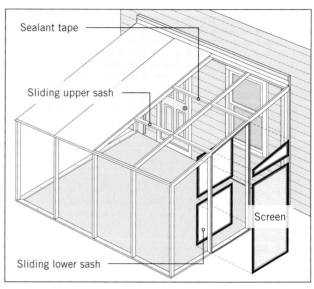

When attaching a sun porch directly to your exterior wall, install 2 × 6 or 2 × 8 edges and hang the roof support beams from it. Also install 2 × 4 vertical nailers beneath the ends of the edges for attaching the walls to the house. Ledgers also may be mounted to rafter ends in the eave area (see previous page).

Sun porch kits with nonglass panels can be mounted on practically any hard surface because they are light enough that they do not require a reinforced floor. You do need to make sure the floor is level, however (see next page), and that the base channels you lay out create square corners.

The Benefits of Roof Ventilation

Without roof vents, hot air is trapped in the sunroom, making it uncomfortable for users and inhospitable to plants.

A single roof vent creates an escape route for hot air, allowing you to regulate the temperature and keep the room cooler during hot weather. Multiple roof vents increase the ventilation efficiency, but increase the chances for leaks.

Options for Anchoring a Sun Porch

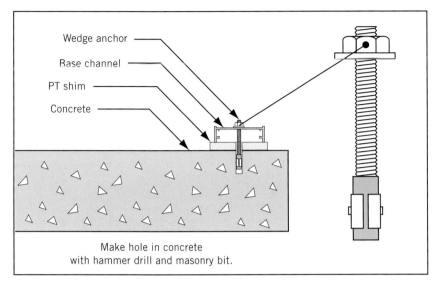

Wedge anchor
Base channel
PT shim
Concrete

Make hole in concrete
with hammer drill and masonry bit.

On concrete patios, attach the base channel to the concrete surface with masonry anchors. There are many styles of anchors you can use. The hardware shown here is a wedge anchor that is driven into a hole drilled through the base channel and into the concrete. If your concrete slab is not level, you'll need to insert shims underneath the base channel in low spots.

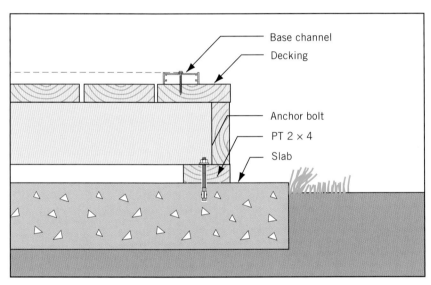

Base channel
Decking
Anchor bolt
PT 2 × 4
Slab

Building a new ground-level deck is a good way to create a stable floor for your sun porch if your concrete patio is in poor condition or if there is no other floor structure in the installation area. Attach pressure-treated 2 × 4 sleepers to the concrete surface to create a raised surface to set the deck on.

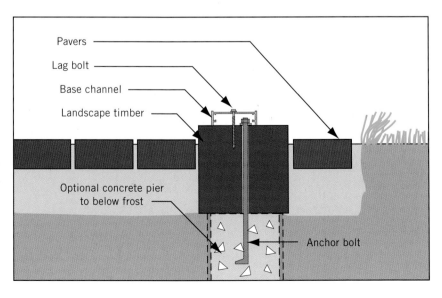

Pavers
Lag bolt
Base channel
Landscape timber
Optional concrete pier
to below frost
Anchor bolt

Set treated wood timbers onto a concrete footing for a sturdy wall base that you can attach to directly when installing the base channels. The footings should extend below your frost line to keep the structure from shifting, but you can use a less permanent floor system, such as sand-set pavers, if you wish.

TOOLS & MATERIALS

4' level
Drill and bits
Hex nut drivers (¼", ⅜")
#2 square screw (Robertson) bit
Socket wrench set
Chalk line

Tape measure
Caulking gun
Rubber mallet
Pressure-treated lumber (2 × 4, 2 × 6)
Exterior house paint
Metal roof flashing

Step ladder
100% silicone caulk
Corrosion-resistant lag screws and washers (¼" × 1½", ¼" × 2½")
Additional fasteners for securing sunroom to house and supporting surface

SUN PORCH TERMS

Mounting surface: May be a level wood deck, concrete slab or patio.

Right and left endwalls: Reference point is with your back to the house looking outwards.

Kneewall (not shown): A site-built wall used to increase the height of the structure.

DOOR INFORMATION

Door (included with kit) may be mounted in any front or endwall bay.

Door opening is 33" wide and 72" high.

Door swings outward and can be hinged for left-hand or right-hand operation.

How to Build a Sun Porch Kit

Install pressure-treated 2 × 4 vertical support cleats and a 2 × 6 horizontal support ledger onto the house wall, following the manufacturer's specifications (See page 125 for options). On nonlap siding, mount the support pieces directly over the siding. For lap siding, cut away the siding and mount the ledger and support cleats over the wall sheathing and building paper. Paint the ledger and cleats before installation, and add roof flashing over the header, leaving it unfastened until the sunroom roof is completely assembled. Make sure the ledger is perfectly level and the vertical cleats are plumb.

COUNTERING SLOPE

Make sure the wood deck, patio, or other installation base is level before installing the sunroom. If not, you may need to install long wood wedges that fit under the floor plates or take other corrective measures as suggested in your installation manual.

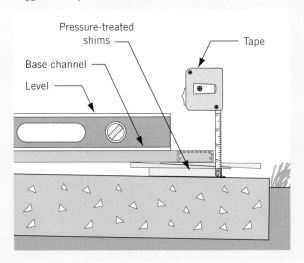

Pressure-treated shims

Tape

Base channel

Level

Lay out the base channel pieces onto your surface in the installation area. Join the pieces using the provided splice brackets and screws. *(continued)*

Position the free ends of the base channel against the wall cleats. Use a 4' level to make sure the channel sections are level. If necessary, use tapered shims to level the channel. Then, check the base frame for square by measuring diagonally from corner to corner. Make adjustments as needed until the measurements are equal.

Fasten the base frame to the surface using a recommended fastener at each of the predrilled mounting holes. Apply a bead of silicone caulk where the channel meets the surface on both sides of the channel. Install the base channel vertical brackets to the base channels using the provided screws (inset photo). These brackets will join the vertical end-wall tubes and front-wall columns to the base channel frame.

To begin assembling the wall and roof structures, first join the endwall headers (the two outside rafters) and the rafters (the interior rafters) to the front-wall columns using the provided mounting brackets and screws. Also install the mounting brackets onto the free ends of the headers and rafters; these are used to mount the headers and rafters to the 2 × 6 support ledger (per step 1 on page 129) on the house wall.

Complete the endwall assemblies by joining the vertical wall tubes to the endwall headers using the provided hardware. Finally, install the mullion brackets onto the sides of the rafters and endwall headers; these will join the horizontal mullions to the rafters and headers to tie the roof frame together (see Step 11).

With a helper, raise one of the endwall assemblies into position and set the vertical tubes over the base channel brackets. Fasten the tubes to the brackets with screws. Install the other endwall assembly the same way.

Anchor the endwall assemblies to the 2 × 4 support cleats and the 2 × 6 support ledger on the house wall. Use a level to position the vertical tubes perfectly plumb, and secure the tubes to the cleats using the recommended fasteners driven through the predrilled holes. Secure the endwall headers to the 2 × 6 support header using the recommended fasteners.

(continued)

Snap a chalk line across the face of the 2 × 6 support ledger so the line is flush with the tops of the endwall headers. This line corresponds to the tops of the rafters and the bottom edge of the top mullion pieces.

Working from one endwall to the other, position the first rafter-front column assembly in place, and secure the column to the base channel using the provided screws. Then, install the horizontal mullions between the endwall header and the first rafter using the provided screws. Repeat this process to install the remaining rafter assemblies and mullions.

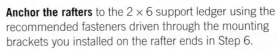

Anchor the rafters to the 2 × 6 support ledger using the recommended fasteners driven through the mounting brackets you installed on the rafter ends in Step 6.

Install the top mullion pieces: Apply silicone caulk to the 2 × 6 support ledger to seal the vertical flange of the top mullions to the ledger. Also caulk where the horizontal flanges of the mullions will meet the endwall headers and rafters. Working from the right endwall to the left, secure the top mullions to the endwall headers and the rafters using the provided screws.

Install the header caps over the tops of the endwall headers; these will help secure the roof glazing panels. First apply a bead of caulk down the center of each header, stopping it 3" from the end of the header. Set each cap into the wet caulk and secure it with the provided screws. Install the rafter caps following the same procedure.

Install the eave mullions over the exposed ends of the rafters and endwall headers. Apply caulk over the center of each frame part and around each predrilled hole. Set the mullions into the wet caulk and secure them with screws.

NOTE: Complete all additional caulking of the framing as recommended by the manufacturer. *(continued)*

Prepare the roofing panels for installation by taping the ends. Cover the top end of each panel with a strip of aluminum tape, and cover the bottom end with vented tape; both tapes are provided. Follow the manufacturers instructions to install any optional roof vents.

Apply adhesive foam gasket strips (provided) to the roof battens that will secure the glazing panels to the roof framing, following the manufacturer's directions. Be careful not to pull or stretch the gaskets. Also apply gaskets to the roof framing, along the endwall headers, rafters, top mullions, and eave mullions, as directed.

Remove the protective film from the first roofing panel, making sure the UV-protected side of the panel is facing up. With a helper, place the panel on top of the endwall header and the adjacent rafter at one end of the roof. The panel should rest against the eave mullion along the front wall.

Secure the outside edge and ends of the panel with the appropriate battens, using the provided screws. To fasten battens to the eave mullion, first drill pilot holes into the mullion, using the predrilled batten holes as a guide. Carefully caulk the panel and battens at the prescribed locations.

Position the next roofing panel onto the rafters, and secure it with battens. The long, vertical batten covers both long edges of the first two panels.

TIP: You have to reach across a panel to fasten vertical battens. This is easiest when you have a tall ladder and use a magnetic nut driver on your drill, which allows you to drive the screws with one hand. Complete the flashing details along the 2 × 6 roof header as directed.

Install the remaining roofing panels, following the same procedure. Be sure to caulk the roofing carefully at all prescribed locations.

(continued)

Begin the wall section installation by adding a triangular aluminum filler piece to the front section of each endwall. Install the fillers with the provided brackets and screws, then caulk along the top and ends of the fillers as directed.

Apply sealant tape along the perimeter of the first section on the front wall. Press the strips of tape firmly together to create a seal at each corner.

TIP: Storing the roll of tape in the refrigerator prior to installation makes it easier to work with.

 TIP

The sunroom's door can go into any one of the wall sections. When choosing the location, plan for easy access to both the house and yard. Also consider how the sunroom's layout will be affected by traffic flow into and out of the door. The door itself always opens out, but it can be hinged on either the right or left side.

23

Determine the door location (see TIP, previous page). Install the first screen/window frame. Set the panel onto the base channel, making sure the frame's weep holes are at the bottom. Align the frame within the opening, and press inward firmly to seat it into the sealant tape. Secure the frame with the provided screws. Install the remaining frames using the same techniques.

24

Install the trapezoidal windows under the headers on the endwalls. Apply sealant tape as before, position the window, then secure it with the provided screws.

(continued)

Complete the window installation by removing the bottom and top sash of each window frame. Peel off the protective film from the glazing, then reinstall each sash, following the manufacturer's directions.

Begin the door installation by fastening the door threshold to the base channel, using the provided screws. Then, add the weatherstripping to the hinge bar and latch bar pieces and the header piece. Trim the excess weatherstripping.

Decide which side of the door will be hinged. Align the hinge bar (with door attached) to the markings on the vertical wall tube or front column, drill pilot holes, and mount the door to the column with screws.

Install the latch bar, leaving a ⅛" gap between the bar and the door edge. Install the header piece, also with a ⅛" gap. Complete the door assembly to add the handle, sweep, and closer, following the manufacturer's instructions.

Apply sealant tape to the door frame, and install the two glazing panels as directed. Add the decorative cover on each side of the door, seating it with a rubber mallet. If the door is located on one of the endwalls, install the trapezoidal window above the door, using the same techniques described in Step 24.

Low-Maintenance Sunroom

TOOLS & MATERIALS

Drill/driver	Roof I-beams
Circular saw	Three-part ridge
Reciprocating saw	pole support
Power miter saw	Ridge pole
Tape measure	(engineered beam)
Caulk gun	Snap-in fascia
Level	Snap-in gutter
Utility knife	with downspouts
Custom wall panels	Moisture-resistant
Custom doors with latches	floor covering
Roof panels	Roof covering (shingles)
Aluminum floor track	Framing lumber
Aluminum vertical	Weatherproof
wall track	silicone sealant
Aluminum upper wall track	Hex-head screws (1", 2", 7")

The term "sunroom" can refer to many different types of rooms, from conservatory-style networks of metal frames and glazing that covers the roof as well as the walls to just about any room in your house that has banks of windows to introduce direct sunlight. The sunroom shown in this project (see Resources, page 236) is a three-season porch that encloses a second-story walk-out deck. The room is a modular kit that was custom-fabricated to the homeowner's exact design and then assembled on site. Except for some custom framing work where the rooflines intersect, the installation was accomplished in a single day.

Built from rigid PVC panels that fit into aluminum frames, this sunroom measures 14 × 14 feet with a 10-foot gable peak. The sidewalls are 7 feet high. The underlying deck area is covered with plywood sheathing that will become a substrate for the finished floor—here, vinyl tiles. The glazing on the windows of the room is a clear vinyl fabric that can stretch to absorb impact and accommodate seasonal changes in framework dimensions.

The installers featured in this project are professional carpenters contracted by the sunroom seller. Custom sunrooms such as this can be ordered and installed by do-it-yourselfers as well. As a percentage of the total package price you won't save a lot by doing the labor yourself, however.

Although they are not seen in the photos, a number of electrical receptacles were installed in the sunroom floor. The feeder cables run back to the house through conduit in the deck joist cavities, because the solid foam panels in the walls and ceilings do not readily accept cables.

To prepare for this new sunroom addition, an old deck was replaced with a new, beefier model. It features a sturdy staircase with enough room on the left side of the addition for an open-air grilling area that is accessed through a door in the sunroom. Instead of decking, the deck area in the sunroom installation area is covered with ¾" tongue-in-groove plywood sheathing.

Before

After

Low-Maintenance Sunroom Kit Parts

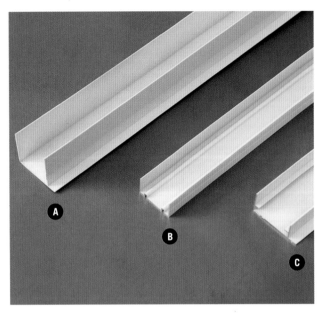

Aluminum tracks secure the prefabricated wall panels. Shown are sections of floor track (A), vertical wall track (B), and upper wall track (C).

Fasteners for this sunroom include self-tapping hex-head screws (1") with low-visibility white heads (A), insulation screws (7") with 2"-dia. fender washers (B), and galvanized self-tapping hex-head screws (2") with self-sealing EPDM rubber washers (C).

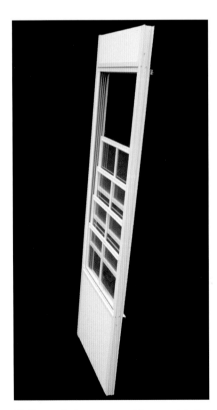

Wall panels for sunroom kits consist of rigid PVC frames with foam insulation in the core. The window sash telescopes downward in four tracks to provide maximum ventilation when open.

Clear vinyl glazing stretches under impact and will not shatter or crack. It is also light enough in weight that sunroom kits often can be installed without structural reinforcement that may be required for units with glass-glazed windows.

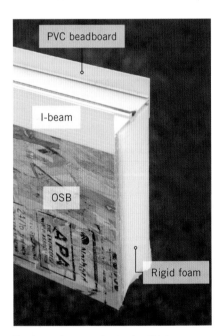

Roof panels come in varying thicknesses depending on the thickness of the rigid foam insulation board that is used (here, 4"). The narrow filler panel seen here features washable PVC beadboard on the interior side to create a ready-to-go ceiling once it is installed. The exterior side of the panel is ⅝" oriented strand board (OSB) to create a surface for installing building paper and asphalt shingles.

How to Install a Low-Maintenance Sunroom

Install the aluminum floor track channels at the perimeter of the installation area. Use a bead of weatherproof silicone sealant and self-tapping, 2" hex-head screws with EPDM rubber washers to secure the track. Square layout lines should be marked prior to installation. If your plywood substrate layer is treated with ACQ or copper azole wood treatment, protect the aluminum tracks from corrosion by installing an isolation layer of PVC flashing (sold in rolls).

PVC flashing (isolation)

Prepare the house walls for installation of the vertical wall tracks. Mark a cutting line on the siding at the track location and remove siding so you can fasten the tracks to the wall sheathing.

TIP: Use a cordless trim saw with a standard blade installed backward to cut vinyl siding.

Remove gutters and other obstructions from the installation area. The exact requirements for this step depend on the configuration of your roof and how you will be tying into the roofline or wall to make space for the sunroom roof.

Install the vertical wall track channels with silicone sealant and self-sealing screws. If the wall sheathing will not accept screws and is not backed by plywood sheathing, you will need to install sturdy wood or wood sheathing backers to secure the track. *(continued)*

Install the first wall panel. In many cases, the first panel will be a narrow filler strip that is simply a solid wall panel and does not contain windows. Install the panel by driving 1" self-tapping screws through the floor track flanges and into the bottom frame of the panel. Make sure the panel is plumb and firmly seated against the track.

Add the next panel according to the installation sequence diagram that comes with your kit. Make sure the panel is plumb and then tack it into position by driving self-tapping screws through the floor flange. The panels lock together at the edges, which will hold them temporarily until the upper wall track can be installed. If you are working in windy conditions, you may need to brace the panels.

Corner post

Filler panel

Upper wall track

Install a corner post at the first corner. The flange on the side of the L-shaped post (inset photo) should capture the end of the first wall's last wall panel. The second wall's first wall panel will fit into the other leg of the L.

Fit the upper wall track over the entire first wall after cutting it to length. The end of the track that joins with the track on the next wall should be mitered to make a neat joint. If the adjoining wall is gabled, this will mean making a relatively tricky compound miter cut. Refer to your plan for the exact angle and don't be shy about asking for help.

Ridge pole post

9

Continue installing panels on the second wall. If it is a gabled wall, install panels up to the midpoint; then cut the three-part, ridge pole support post to fit, and install it by driving screws through the post and into the wall panel. Make sure the saddle formed at the top of the post is sized to accept the ridge pole.

10

Install the remaining wall panels, creating corners and adding upper wall tracks as you go. Frequently check for plumb and level, and make sure all panels are seated firmly in the tracks.

11

Mark the upper wall tracks at the gable for cutting by transferring the edges of the ridge pole saddle onto the ends of tracks. Cut them to length and the correct angle with a power miter saw and metal cutting blade. Or, you can use an old combination blade that you don't mind making dull.

12

Ridge pole

Set the ridge pole into the saddle in the ridge pole post, and adjust it until the overhang is correct. Check the length: if the pole does not end at the correct point on the other end, recut it or adjust your overhang amount. Secure the end by driving screws through the ridge pole post and into the ridge pole.

(continued)

Secure the house-end of the ridge pole. Begin by installing a temporary post near the house wall that is the same height as the bottom of the saddle opening in the ridge pole post. Make sure the ridge pole is level and then measure for attaching it to the house. The exact method you use depends on the house structure. Here, the exterior wall that will support the ridge is set back 18" from a pair of bay windows that are covered by the same roof. This means that the cap plate for the bearing wall that will support the ridge pole is lower than the bottom of the pole. The distance is measured (left photo) and a 2 × 6 half-lap post anchor is constructed. The anchor is nailed to the cap plate on the wall and then the ridge pole is attached to the anchor with deck screws (right photo).

Begin installing roof panels. The full-width panels seen here are 4' wide, yet they are strong enough to meet minimum dead load ("snow") requirements even in cold climates. The panels are attached with long insulation screws that are fitted with fender washers and driven into the ridge pole and upper wall track.

Install I-beams on the roof next to the first roof panel. The track on one side of the I-beam should capture the leading edge of the first roof panel. Attach the I-beam to the roof panel with self-tapping screws driven through the I-beam flange and down into the OSB panel surface.

(16)

Add the next roof panel to the roof, sliding it into the open side of the I-beam. Square the panel with the roof, and then drive insulation screws down through the panel and into the ridge pole and the upper wall track. Add the next I-beam and fasten it with self-tapping screws.

Continue installing panels and I-beams until the roof is complete. Complete one full side before beginning the other.

(17)

(18)

Gutter

Install fascia and gutters. The materials seen here are designed specifically to work with the roof panel system of this kit. The fascia snaps over the ends of the roof panels and is secured with screws. The gutters fit into tracks on the fascia and are secured with screws.

(19)

Install the prehung doors by fastening the door nailing flanges to the frames that create the door opening. Make sure the door is level and plumb before driving fasteners. Attach the door handle and latch.

(20)

Make finishing touches, such as trimming off excess insect screening and painting or cladding the ridge pole. If your sunroom does not have a finished ceiling, add one (tongue-and-groove cedar carsiding is a good choice). Install floorcoverings.

Special Section: Upcycled Greenhouses & Cold Frames

The best greenhouse or cold frame is a free one—and one that doesn't use up valuable natural resources. Repurposing waste materials into a backyard plant-growing structure is a common-sense approach for the environment and your pocketbook, keeping waste out of the landfill and putting it to an ecologically productive use. It doesn't hurt that reusing waste materials can also mean saving a bundle of money. Along the way, you may well expand your gardening repertoire.

There are many ways to upcycle materials into a greenhouse or other plant-care structure. The first step, though, is to understand exactly what "upcycling" means.

Upcycling is the more efficient cousin to recycling. Recycling involves using a lot of energy to break waste materials, such as plastic bottles, down into their fundamental ingredients and reform those ingredients into new consumer goods (or even the same consumer goods). Upcycling, on the other hand, is reusing waste materials in their current forms as building blocks for something completely different. This isn't a new or novel concept—the back-to-the-land movement and homesteaders across the country have been turning one man's trash into another's treasure for decades.

The variety of "trash" that can be upcycled for use as cold frames, greenhouses, hoophouses, or similar garden structures is simply astounding. The structural principles behind greenhouses and cold frames naturally lend themselves to building with a host of repurposed materials. The creative gardener can upcycle straw bales, plastic bottles, old windows, old tires, and even pruned tree branches.

Where to Start

You need look no further than the local landfill to see how the volume of our waste material is overwhelming our ability to contain it. Efficient reuse of that material starts with filling a need. Looking to build a full-blown greenhouse from reclaimed waste? That will probably entail finding an outside source for reclaimed lumber and old windows. But if your needs are more modest—such as a cloche, a simple cold frame, or even a quick and easy raised bed—everything you require may be right in your own backyard, in the recycling bin, or the back of the garage. Plastic gallon jugs, plumbing odds and ends, and lumber scraps can all be efficiently upcycled. Once you've got an idea of the structure or structures you want to build, it's time to search for the appropriate raw materials.

The ideal is always "free." Check Craigslist (craigslist.org), the Freecycle Network (freecycle. org), and the postings on local co-op or community bulletin boards for free materials. The best source for free upcycle materials is the most unpleasant: dumpster diving. Look behind large stores for discarded pallets. Check the dumpsters at large-scale demo projects—such as a tear-down of a

UPCYCLING RULES

The rules of upcycling are simple and straightforward.

1. Don't scavenge from private property.

2. Safety first. Don't use unsafe materials or methods, and don't create unsafe structures from upcycled materials.

3. Don't create more waste than you reuse.

4. Use whatever materials you recycle in as close to original form as possible.

5. The end product must have a functional purpose.

condemned building. You'll find usable wood, old windows, and possibly even plumbing scraps on the worksites of major remodeling projects. (Always ask before going into a dumpster on private property or a job site.)

If you can't find the material you need for free, you can often buy it at very low cost. Check the local Yellow Pages for salvage companies, or visit local Habitat ReStore outlets.

CULTIVATION UNDER CLOCHE

Greenhouses, cold frames, and hoophouses are all fine for entire beds or large areas of the garden, but if you want to protect just one or a few plants, a cloche can be the perfect solution. *Cloche* is the French word for "bell," and the first cloches were bell-shaped glass jars that produce-market vendors used to grow vegetables out of season for Parisian restaurants and farmers' markets. Today, manufacturers offer many lightweight, low-cost versions, from basic plastic "solar bells" to aluminum-and-plastic lantern cloches. But really, a plastic milk jug or liter bottle will do the job just as well. In addition, the screw-top lid on most plastic bottles gives a bit more control over how hot the plant gets. (In a traditional cloche, you prop up the side to vent and cool the plant.) Keep in mind, however, that no matter what you use as a cloche, it's meant to simply extend the frost date of the plant, not grow it throughout the winter.

The Materials

If you use your imagination, almost anything in the garbage can find a purpose elsewhere. But some materials are naturally better suited to repurposing for greenhouses and gardens than others.

Plastic bottles: There is an epidemic of plastic bottles in America. Vastly more are produced than are recycled, and they constitute much of the waste quickly filling landfills (not to mention covering the ocean). Bottle plastic doesn't break down, so if a bottle isn't reused or recycled, it will remain forever wherever it lands. But the translucent structure and the fact that plastic doesn't breathe make this material ideal for repurposing in the garden. Plastic bottles can be used as simple cloches (see the box on page 150), filled with poor-quality soil, dirt, or other material and stacked to create garden walls, and even used in the walls of a greenhouse. The bad news about bottles is also good news for upcyclers: they're everywhere, and few people will complain if you collect them from recycling or garbage bins! (Make sure this is not illegal in your community; in some locales, recycled materials are a revenue stream for the civil government.)

Pallets: Used wherever goods are transported in bulk (which is to say everywhere), pallets are almost as ubiquitous as plastic bottles. One broken board or cracked brace means a pallet is unusable for its intended purpose, but it may still be usable for your greenhouse. Pallets can be used whole, as a solid, level surface that can serve as the floor or workbench of a greenhouse, or they can be modified and used to make potting tables, garden chairs, and even side walls for a greenhouse. Avoid using pallets that have been treated with preservatives, fungicides, or other

Plastic bottles have largely become an environmental disaster. But they can be put to good use in the garden, protecting small, vulnerable plants from cold snaps and extreme temperature variations. The cap provides a vent that allows you to release hot air and humidity as necessary.

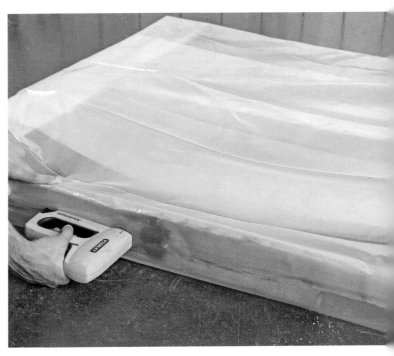

Modifying a pallet like this—removing the center rails and replacing them with 6-mil polyethylene sheeting—is one of the many ways you can upcycle these handy throwaways. This crude "window" can be used as a building block to form walls and a roof for a greenhouse.

chemicals, and avoid those with paint on them if you can. On the other hand, keep an eye out for the mark "HT"—that stands for "Heat Treated," which means the pallet has been processed to kill any pathogens.

Wood: Old fence wood, rescued deck boards, discarded clapboard siding, and broken lumber can all benefit the garden. Reclaimed wood can be used in greenhouses, cold frames, and many other structures. The chances are that you'll have to adapt the wood to your purpose, but a little sanding, ripping, or sawing is a small price to pay for free wood. Even wood scraps can be handy. Leftover 2 × 4 sections can be laminated together to form long 4 × 4 timbers for greenhouse foundations, skids, or raised bed walls. Cut down damaged 2× wood for the slotted tops of greenhouse workbenches or to use as stakes for the frame of a hoophouse.

If you're reclaiming wood from a much older building or any that has been around for decades, keep in mind that the wood may be actual size rather than nominal size—in other words, what looks like a 4 × 4 may actually be 4 inches by 4 inches, rather than 3½ inches by 3½ inches. That may mean adjusting building plans. Be leery of any wood that might have been treated with chemicals. For instance, old railroad track ties were once quite popular for garden bed borders, until gardeners realized that most of these have been treated with toxic, heavy-metal-based preservatives. The best woods to reclaim are naturally pest- and rot-resistant varieties—specifically cedar and redwood, or any hardwood.

Windows: Old windows are obvious choices for crafting a greenhouse or cold frame. It's fairly easy to find old storm windows or double-hung units that have been replaced with insulated windows. Look on Craigslist, or touch base with local window contractors. The one drawback is that you can never be sure of what size you'll get, so be ready to adapt your plans. Wood-framed windows are the easiest to upcycle because it's much simpler to drill, saw, or modify wood. Metal and vinyl frame windows can work, but you'll need carbide drill bits and a bit more patience. Single-pane windows without mullions are the best option, because they cast the least amount of shadow on plants. If you're using reclaimed windows for a greenhouse, you'll also want the windows to be as airtight as possible; your garden may be better served if you take a little time and recaulk the windows before integrating them into a cold frame or greenhouse.

Tires: Discarded car and truck tires represent an environmental disaster. Not only do they take up a lot of room in landfills (and in many unofficial, illegal dumpsites), they are also slow to break down. Worse still, waste tires represent a significant fire hazard. The good news? It's not hard to find discarded tires, and you can put them to work with little effort. The thick rubber surface of even worn tires is a great insulator. It also absorbs and holds heat, making it a fantastic choice for a raised bed in a greenhouse, where it will absorb heat all day and release it slowly at night.

A tire is also a great way to protect a tender plant or plants. Make a crude cold frame out of a tire by

You don't have to look far to find secondhand wood that can be reused in garden structures, but take steps to ensure old, potentially toxic paint and finishes are removed before you upcycle reclaimed wood.

Old, discarded windows are the environmentally conscious greenhouse gardener's treasure. They can easily be turned into a simple cold frame, or combined to create a nearly free greenhouse.

A used tire makes a wonderful raised bed that can be placed where it is most convenient for the gardener. Inside a greenhouse, the rubber becomes a heat sink that releases heat after the sun goes down.

Reclaimed granite "curbstones" can serve as a tremendous foundation for a permanent greenhouse. They also make attractive walls for raised beds.

placing it over a plant and topping it with an old window (cut away the side walls with a reciprocating saw to increase the planting area). Lay the window across the tire and use a bolster to prop it up when you need to ventilate or cool the plant (or just cover the top with plastic sheet secured with bricks).

You can also use a tire as a quick and easy potato bed. Fill the tire with soil and plant the seed potatoes. When the first growth breaks through the surface, stack another tire on top and fill with soil.

Buckets: Buckets, specifically 5-gallon buckets, are used to hold everything from bulk food ingredients to drywall compound and much more. They are also incredibly durable and won't break down in landfills. You can use buckets as beds for deep-rooted plants and even tree saplings, and they also make effective heat sinks. Paint the bucket black, fill it with water, and let the sun warm it all day; at night, it will slowly release heat, preventing the greenhouse from cooling too fast or too much.

Stones: All kinds of reclaimed stone and brick can be put to good use in the greenhouse and garden. Use flagstone or brick—especially darker colors—for the floor of a greenhouse to incorporate a natural heat sink. A brick or stone floor is also a stunning addition to any greenhouse and one that creates a stable surface on which to stand and work. You can make wonderfully eye-catching raised beds inside or outside of a greenhouse with field stones or other irregularly shaped, uncut stones. A black bucket filled with river rock or trap stone can be an efficient heat sink.

It might look like a chaotic mess of plumbing leftovers, but this is actually a cold frame or greenhouse frame just waiting to be rescued and assembled.

Plumbing pipe: A pile of old plumbing pipe and connectors might look like a mess, but look again. Plastic pipe can be used to fashion hoophouses and row cover frames. Old metal plumbing pipes and elbows can be repurposed into frames for cold frames and even for greenhouses. Any pipe can be crafted into a serviceable trellis to use along the back wall of a greenhouse for vining or tall-growing plants.

Upcycled Projects

Separating your recyclables and putting them out in the proper bin on the proper day is certainly an environmentally conscientious step in the right direction. But the rubber really hits the road when you put waste materials to work in your own garden so that they never enter the waste stream and no fuel is burned in transportation or the recycling process itself.

The projects that follow use a range of reclaimed materials in some surprisingly innovative ways. You can take these right off the page and build them yourself or use them as points of departure for imagining new projects that reuse your remodeling leftovers and garage debris. In either case, keep in mind that even as you break down materials to make them work for the structure you're building, the scraps are reusable. Cutting down a PVC pipe for a hoophouse? Cut the scraps into stakes to use for a raised bed. Have leftover lumber that's too short to use for framing or a greenhouse floor? Keep it handy for when you want to build shelves or a small potting table.

An old window (or two) is the perfect partner for straw bales, creating an easy, quick, and efficient cold frame. Construct the cold frame so the face is sloped to face the best sun exposure.

 A STRAW-BALE COLD FRAME

Straw bales are growing in popularity as a medium for gardening, but they can also serve as excellent insulated walls for a cold-weather cold frame that you can assemble in minutes and move at a whim.

There are several ways to create the cold frame, but in every case, you start by building a stepped frame with a shorter wall on the south side. Then it's just a matter of deciding on your glazing material, which can be a totally opportunistic decision. For example, do you have an old single-pane window that you meant to take to the dump? Don't. Lay it with one long edge resting on the north wall of your bales, nestled into between the two side walls. Prop the window up as necessary to vent or cool down the plants inside. You can use the same idea with a role of plastic sheeting over a plumbing pipe or lumber scrap frame—just roll the sheet up or down as needed to modulate the temperature inside the cold frame.

USING CLEAR PLASTIC BOTTLES FOR GREENHOUSE PANELS

Building panels out of plastic bottles may be a bit labor intensive, but it's a perfect upcycle use. Passive solar panels made from ordinary clear plastic bottles can be used for everything from a top cover for a cold frame box to the entire wall and roof panels for full greenhouse. No matter what the scale, it's also a wonderful school project or weekend event for a group of kids because the actual work itself is so simple, plus it's a hands-on way to teach them the importance of recycling and reusing. The more kids, the merrier.

Start by collecting the bottles you need. It's easy to find them in abundance in curbside recycling bins on collection day, inside the dumpsters in back of restaurants, or in the garbage cans at outdoor music events or other public gatherings. (As noted previously, make sure this is legal where you live.)

It's essential to clean the bottles inside and out to avoid attracting insects. Strip any labels off the plastic to ensure that a maximum amount of light passes through.

Begin by creating whatever kind of frame for greenhouse structure you're planning. At the large end of the scale, you can frame out a simple gable or shed-roof greenhouse using reclaimed wood, scraps leftover from other projects, or other material you have on hand. The greenhouse shouldn't be large—the finished project will have too many gaps for air and water penetration for the structure to function as a fully fledged greenhouse. However, on sunny days, it will be able to maintain an interior temperature about 40 degrees warmer than the outside air.

Once you have built whatever frame you are using, you can begin assembling the simple columns that will compose various panels. You can use poles made from ¾-inch to 1-inch dowels, leftover metal conduit, bamboo canes, straight and thin branches, rebar, or even wire. No matter what you make them from, the poles need to be long enough to span the frame members.

Cut the bottoms of the bottles off and thread them onto the pole, nesting each additional bottle over the one below. Attached the completed poles to the framing at each end with pipe clamps.

As mentioned, the resulting surfaces will necessarily have gaps, but the cumulative effect of the enclosure will be to allow light through while keeping temperatures high.

Once you cut the bottoms off of the plastic bottles, they'll stack easily on whatever you're using for a pole. In our example, the plastic-bottle panel will be used as a simple cold-frame top to cover a small raised bed garden.

Old-Window Greenhouse

Old, discarded windows are just about the most obvious choice for reuse in upcycled greenhouses. As homeowners across the country upgrade to insulated windows, older windows are relegated to the junk heap. These include wood-framed units that have seen better days, aluminum-framed storm windows that are no longer needed, and even vinyl-clad insulated windows that have come to the end of their lifespan. You can find them in dumpsters, piled up on remodeling job sites, for sale cheaply through salvage companies, and online through various sources—often for free.

The trick to reusing these windows for a greenhouse is that you have to take what you get. Sizes vary, sometimes radically. The design shown here is typical, featuring a small footprint and a simple shed roof. The recycled windows used are 28 inches wide by 62 inches high; the larger windows are used in the walls, and the smaller are used in the roof. In both cases, these instructions assume wood-framed units. Wood framing is always best when it comes to adapting old glazing to a new hobby greenhouse, but you have to make sure that the wood is in good shape. The lumber used is all of common sizes and should be readily available through salvage companies or from job sites. The design can be scaled up or adapted to different sizes of windows fairly easily, as the framing details have intentionally been left somewhat crude to allow adaptation without a lot of fuss. A kneewall base ensures that no matter what windows you reuse, they'll be well supported. We've also used fiberglass panels, which are widely available and simple to install, for the roof.

When creating a design such as this, using mostly recycled materials, it's a great idea to lay the windows and framing studs out on a big, flat work surface—for example, a garage floor or expanse of lawn. If you're not necessarily good with the nitty-gritty of detailed measurements and nominal lumber sizes, this can be a way to verify that everything will fit and to make quick adjustments without having to tear things apart. Whatever the case, it's always wisest to try to find multiple windows in the same size; cobbling together windows of odd sizes throughout the structure can lead to a nightmare and create an unstable and unsafe greenhouse.

That said, any upcycling project involves certain compromises. This greenhouse will not be as airtight as most polycarbonate panel or plastic-film kit greenhouses would be (and certainly not as much of a high-quality custom structure), so it is at best going to serve you as a three-season structure—it just wouldn't be cost effective to heat it over a cold winter. You can make the structure a little more efficient by recaulking the window panes in wood-framed windows and covering smaller openings or gaps between the windows in the roof and the wall top plates with plastic.

TOOLS & MATERIALS

Cordless power drill and bits	Stepladder	Finish nails	Level
Claw hammer	Clear silicone caulk	Circular saw	Speed square
Paintbrush	Construction adhesive	12" spikes	Wood screws (2½", 3")
Sealant or paint	Caulk gun	Jigsaw	1" screws
	Nails (6d, 8d)	Tamper	Rubber washers

Build a greenhouse of old windows and you not only save money, but you also create a distinctive structure that puts a dumpster worth of waste materials to great use.

How to Build an Old-Window Greenhouse

Inspect all of the windows for significant defects you might have missed during the reclaiming process. Look for rust, excessive warping, and hidden insect damage or rot (if you're using wood-framed units). Clean up the windows and sand or use a wire wheel to remove loose or flaking finishes or rough areas. Paint the frames with primer or coat with preservative. Fasten the 4 × 4 frame together by joining the timbers at the corner with 12" spikes, countersunk. Measure and mark the trenches for 4 × 4 foundation timbers. Dig them 4" deep and fill with crushed gravel. Tamp the gravel down all around.

Check the frame for level on all sides, side by side, and diagonally. Add or remove gravel under the foundation to level any one side.

Working on a clean, flat surface such as the lawn here, lay out and build one side wall. Nail the sole and top plates to the studs after ensuring that each stud is at a 45° angle to the plate with a speed square.

(4)

Raise the wall, check for plumb, and brace it into position. Nail the sole plate to the foundation timber with 8d nails.

(5)

Once the two side walls are constructed and nailed in position, build and raise the rear (nondoor) wall into place and nail it to the foundation 4 × 4.

(6)

Screw the walls together at the corners with 3" wood screws.

(7)

Screw 2 × 4 × 28¼" spreaders in the stud cavities of the side and back walls. Toe-screw the spreaders on the inside edges and face-screw through the corners (inset). The tops of spreaders should be 32" above the 4 × 4 base, faces flush with the outside edges of the wall studs. *(continued)*

Face-nail a 2 × 4 cedar ledger around the perimeter of the greenhouse so that the top of the ledger is flush with the tops of the 2 × 4 spreaders.

Use a jigsaw to cut notches in 5/4 cedar decking to use as window sills on top of the spreaders.

Dry-fit the cedar sills and then miter the corners if the fit is correct. Coat the tops of the spreaders with construction adhesive and nail the cedar sills in place with exterior finish nails.

11

Miter-cut retainer strips from ¾" quarter-round stock for the window openings. Drill pilot holes for nailing, then coat the bottom faces of the strips with construction adhesive and nail them in place with exterior finish nails. You may have to adjust for the windows you reclaim. The windows here varied in height by up to ½".

12

Lay a thin bead of clear silicone caulk into the retainer strip channel for the first window.

13

With a helper, carefully and evenly set the window into position. Have the helper hold the window in place for the next step.

14

Pin the window in place with small brads to allow the silicone to set. Repeat the installation process with the rest of the windows for the three walls. *(continued)*

Measure and cut 2 × 6 fascia boards for the top of each wall. Use 3" 6d galvanized nails to tack the board to the top plates of the wall all the way around. The fascia should cover any gaps at the tops of the windows.

Measure and cut 1 × 3 cedar strips to run between the fascia at the top and the sill. Drill pilot holes and nail the strips in place on the studs with 3" 6d nails.

Measure and cut ½" exterior grade plywood for the half-wall cladding at the bottom of each wall. Nail it in place with 2" 6d nails.

Measure and cut 2 × 4 cedar base trim, 1 × 3 cedar corner boards, and 1 × 3 cedar battens. Nail them in place with exterior finish nails, positioning the battens between the base trim and the underside of the sill, continuing the vertical line of the stile trim.

Frame the front wall (12" higher than the side walls) in place by measuring and marking stud and doorjamb positions and toe-nailing the members in place. Nail the top cap to the top of the studs and install the door header. Install the door so that it opens outward.

Use 2½" deck screws to toe-screw the front cripple studs for the triangular top walls on both sides.

Measure and cut the other cripple studs in each top wall and toe-screw them in place with 2½" deck screws. Check that each is plumb and square to the top plate. Miter each end of the top plates and screw them to the cripple studs on each wall.

Measure and cut the 2 × 4 rafters and toe-screw them running front wall to back wall. There should be a 6" overhang on both ends.

Measure and cut the 2 × 2 purlins for the gaps between the rafters. Toe-screw them in place, spaced 11½" on center.

Cut and screw the fiberglass panel nailing strips to the top of each purlin.

Drill pilot holes for the fiberglass panels and screw them in place to the purlins using 1" screws and rubber washers. Paint or stain the exterior of the greenhouse and, if using in a cooler season, cover all the clerestory windows with 6–8 mil plastic sheeting stapled in place.

Old-Window Portable Cold Frame

A simple, portable cold frame can be incredibly useful in the early-spring garden (or, in some cases, the late-fall garden). Depending on where you live, you'll realize an extra six to eight weeks of growing time—a chance to get a big head start on your garden and harden off seedlings.

This cold frame will do the job well without taking a bite out of your pocketbook. It is built with reclaimed 1 × 6 cedar fence boards and scrap pressure-treated 2 × 4 braces, and the top is a 24 × 36-inch salvaged wood-frame window. But keep in mind that you can use this design as a baseline; this is somewhat smaller than most cold frames, which makes it more portable, but it may not be suited to a large garden bed. It's easy to alter the measurements to suit whatever window you happen to use—or even a glass door. You can also use a vinyl-clad window or aluminum-framed unit, although they will both make the box less attractive in the garden. Or, for a sturdier box, use 2 × 6 reclaimed lumber. That will make the cold frame much less portable but better suited to take abuse from the elements, pets, and small children.

The design here includes mitered top edges along the length of the front and back frame members, which allows the window to close flush to the surface. If you aren't equipped to make those miters or just prefer to avoid the extra work, switch the frame configuration so that the sides are positioned inside the front and back frames. The window top will still close along the slope, although the seal on the front and back will be slightly less secure.

TOOLS & MATERIALS

Tape measure	(1) stainless-steel sash handle	Sandpaper
Table saw or jigsaw	2" galvanized screws	Caulk
Power drill and bits	6d galvanized nails	Paint
(3) 4" galvanized T-hinges	Speed square	Paintbrush

Why build just one old-window cold frame when you can build an entire bank of them, like this greenhouse owner did?

CUTTING LIST

KEY	PART	NO.	DIMENSION	MATERIAL
A	Sloped side frame	2	¾ × 5¼ × 23¼"	Cedar
B	Side frame base	2	¾ × 5¼ × 23¼"	Cedar
C	Front & back frame	3	¾ × 5¼ × 34½"	Cedar
D	Rear frame posts	2	1½ × 3½ × 10½"	PT
E	Front frame posts	2	1½ × 3½ × 7"	PT

This old-window cold frame can be built with materials found on most any home renovation site, or you may even have them in the back of your garage or basement.

Inspect a 1 × 6 fence board, at least 24" long, to ensure that it is straight and free of defects. Measure from one corner, down 24" to the bottom edge of the board, creating a right-angle triangle. Use a speed square to mark a straight line up from the bottom point of the triangle (the lower tip of the hypotenuse). Cut the board along the marked lines to make the sloped tops of the side frames.

Stand a rear frame board with the face flush to the back edge of the sloped side frame piece. Mark the angled bevel cut on the edge of the rear frame board. Repeat the process with the front frame board.

Use a table saw adjusted to the correct angle, or a jigsaw set to the miter, to bevel-cut the top edges of the front and back frame boards. Drill pilot holes in the edges of the framing pieces, two for each board, at each joint. Tack the frame together with 6d common nails. Check to make sure that the window you've reclaimed fits the frame perfectly and make any adjustments if it does not.

Hold each back post in place and mark a cutting line along the sloped side frame. Do the same with the front posts. Use a table saw or handsaw and miter box to make the angled cuts on each post.

Drill pilot holes and screw the posts in place in each corner of the box.

Clean up the window, sanding rough spots as necessary, and recaulking the window if needed. Prime and paint the window (paint it a darker color to absorb heat during the day and release it at night).

Mark the placement of the three hinges and screw them to the window frame and rear box frame. Measure and mark for the sash handle on the front of the frame and screw it in place. If desired, cut a 1× scrap piece to about 15" long to use as a support post to hold the window open when you work in the cold frame.

Tree Branch Hoophouse

This rudimentary structure bridges the gap between a full-blown greenhouse and a simple hoop-row cover frame. It follows many of the guiding principles of the Old-Window Greenhouse (page 156)—it's lightweight, it's easy to assemble, it uses mostly upcycled components, and it should be exceedingly inexpensive to build.

There are tradeoffs, of course. This hoophouse is somewhat less durable than it would be if it were made with PVC hoops and thicker, clear, new lumber. If durability is important to you, you might want to upgrade to 2× lumber in place of the 1× members specified, and it would definitely be a good idea to anchor the hoophouse if you live in a region where strong winds or curious wildlife are factors.

The goal throughout is to make the most of scraps and project odds and ends. You may have even better ideas than the upcycled materials specified in this project. Don't be afraid to be imaginative. The baseboards may come from old deck fascia, torn-down fences, or clapboard siding from a defunct building. Branches serve as the hoops, and they will probably be the most challenging building material to find. If you don't have mature trees that need pruning in your yard, you can usually find suitable branches in a forest or woods. (Consider it a good reason for a hike!) If possible, look for ideal branches are at least 10 feet long, green enough to be supple and flexible, and roughly the same diameter all along their length. Ideal branches are hard to find, though, and it is perfectly acceptable to form each hoop from shorter branches bent over from each side and lashed together at the top. This is the method used in our example.

Don't be fooled by the modest footprint of this hoophouse. There is enough room inside to grow an ample bed of edibles or ornamentals, and the height allows for tall plants. If, however, you'd prefer to cover a larger area, it's simple to scale the structure up. Just increase it in foot increments, adding one branch hoop per foot.

TOOLS & MATERIALS

Level

Scissors

Tape measure

Circular saw

Hacksaw

Power drill and bits

2" galvanized screws

Loppers

Sandpaper

(4) 1" steel round conduit brackets

(20) galvanized pipe clamps (sized to match PCV stakes)

Zip ties

Wood mallet

Staple gun and staples

2 rolls 6-mil polyethylene sheeting

Look for green, freshly cut branches ¾ to 1" in diameter. If you can find 10-footers, that's perfect; otherwise, lash shorter ones together as shown in this project.

A simple hoophouse like this, formed of branches and reclaimed lumber, can be a wonderful addition to any garden for little or no cost.

Clear the hoophouse site of large rocks and yard debris. On a clean, flat surface, assemble the base frame by drilling pilot holes through the frame edges and screwing the frame together with 2" galvanized screws. Cut individual branches with loppers to length as necessary. Cut off or sand down any protrusions that might puncture the plastic.

Use a hacksaw to cut the PVC pipe scraps to 8" long (they can be longer, but not shorter). Cut one end of each pipe scrap on the diagonal at a severe angle to create a stake point.

Attach the PVC pipes to the inside frame faces, spacing them 1' apart. Use two pipe strap clamp brackets per pipe. The pipes should project about 1" above the top edge of the frame side.

Move the base frame to the final site. Check that the frame is level and square by measuring diagonals and adjust as necessary. Use a wood mallet to hammer the PVC stakes into the ground, alternating sides, until the frame is secure.

Install the branch hoops by placing one end of each branch in a PVC stake and slowly bending the other ends across the top. Secure the branches together at the top with several zip ties. The branches should hold securely in the stakes with friction, but if any of them wants to pop out, drive a screw through the side of the PVC stake and into the branch.

Lay the ridge pole along the top edge of the frame base side and mark the positions of the PVC pipe stakes on the branch. Cut slight notches at the marks with a jigsaw. Lay the ridge branch across the hoops so they fit into the notches and zip-tie the hoops to the ridge pole.

Position each front and back support in place with one end against the ground on the inside of the frame and the other against the end hoops. Mark cutting lines where the end hoops intersect the tops of the supports, then cut the front and back supports to fit. Screw the front and back supports to the frame at the bottoms, and secure the top to the hoops with conduit brackets.

Drape the hoops with the plastic sheeting. Cut the sheet to fit, then either double-fold the edges and staple them to the base frame or let them flow over onto the ground and secure them with bricks. Cut a smaller piece of plastic to use as a door flap, and staple it into place.

Bamboo Trellis

Bamboo is an ideal material for building custom trellises and other structures to support climbing plants in your greenhouse. Bamboo poles are lightweight, strong, and naturally decay-resistant. And because it's a giant grass and in its natural form, bamboo looks right at home in any greenhouse.

In this easy project, you'll learn the traditional technique of constructing with natural bamboo poles and lashing twine. The trellis shown is freestanding and is held upright with rebar rods driven into the ground. It's easy enough to find bamboo in plentiful amounts because it's rugged and invasive. The thin canes you need for this project should be simple to come by (we painted the bamboo in this project red to show detail), although if you can't find any, you'll be able to buy the bamboo.

Bamboo poles are sold through online retailers, local bamboo suppliers (where available), import stores, and some garden centers. The poles come in sizes ranging from about ¼ to 5 inches in diameter and in lengths up to 20 feet or so. Of course, the diameters are approximate and variable, since this is a natural product. For this project, the vertical supports are 1½ inches in diameter and the horizontal and vertical crosspieces are 1 inch in diameter.

While bamboo can survive many years of exposure to the elements, a bamboo trellis is lightweight enough that you can simply pull it off of its supports and store it over winter. Ground contact or burial of bamboo poles does lead to premature rot, so it's a good idea to prop up the trellis poles on stones or brick to prevent ground contact. A small pile of stones nicely hides the rebar and creates an attractive base around each support pole.

A bamboo trellis like this is great for bolstering any climbing plant. You can build a taller version for pole beans and other aggressive climbers or add more crosspieces or weave kite string between poles to support delicate vines.

TOOLS & MATERIALS

Tape measure	Pencil	(2) 5' bamboo poles (1"-dia.)	2' length of #2 rebar or metal rod
Hacksaw	Level	(4) 4' bamboo poles (1"-dia.)	Stones
Hammer	Waxed lashing twine	(3) 3' lengths of #3 rebar	Eye and ear protection
Scissors	(3) 5' bamboo poles (1½"-dia.)		Work gloves
Hand maul			

How to Build a Bamboo Trellis

Trim off the top end of each vertical pole just above a node, using a hacksaw. The solid membrane of the node will serve as a cap to prevent water from collecting inside the pole. Trim the three 1½"-diameter vertical support poles and four 1"-diameter vertical crosspieces.

Node

Measuring from the trimmed top ends of the vertical poles, cut the two outer support poles to length at 48", and cut the four vertical crosspieces at 36". The middle support pole and horizontal crosspieces should be about 60" long; cut them to length only if necessary.

Break out the nodes in the bottom ends of the three vertical support poles, using a hammer and #2 rebar or other metal rod, shaking out the broken pieces as you work. Remove any nodes within the bottom 18" of each pole.

TIP: If the first node is close to the end, it might help to drill several holes through the node before breaking it out.

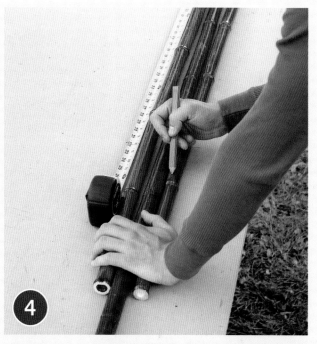

Mark the poles for positioning, using a pencil; these are layout marks that represent the pole intersections. Mark the vertical support poles at 12" and 36" from the bottom ends. On each horizontal crosspiece, make a mark at the center and at 6", 14", and 22" from each end. Finally, make a mark at 6" from each end of the vertical crosspieces.

(continued)

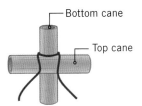
Bottom cane
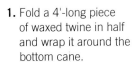
Top cane

1. Fold a 4'-long piece of waxed twine in half and wrap it around the bottom cane.

2. Pull both ends of the twine across the top cane and cross them underneath the bottom cane.

3. Pull the twine ends back up and cross them over the top cane.

4. Cross the twine underneath the joint, forming an X.

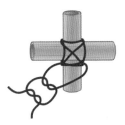

5. Lift the ends up and make an X across the top of the joint.

6. Wrap the bottom cane from below and then across the top, next to the joint.

7. Wrap the bottom cane on the other side of the joint.

8. Tie a square knot and then trim off the twine ends.

Lay out the poles onto a flat work surface, starting with the vertical support poles. To facilitate the lashing process, let the bottom ends of the poles overhang the edge of the work surface beyond the lower layout marks. Position the bottom horizontal crosspiece on top of the support poles using the layout marks for positioning.

Lash the crosspiece to each support pole, using a 60"-long piece of waxed lashing twine; see LASHING TECHNIQUE, above. When each lashing is complete, trim the excess twine with scissors.

Lash the remaining horizontal crosspiece at the upper marks on the support poles. Position the vertical crosspieces on top of the horizontals, and lash the poles together at each intersection.

Position the completed trellis framework in the desired location of the garden or planting bed. The back sides of the vertical support poles should face away from the planting area. Press down on the framework so the vertical support poles make an impression in the soil, marking the locations of the rebar spikes.

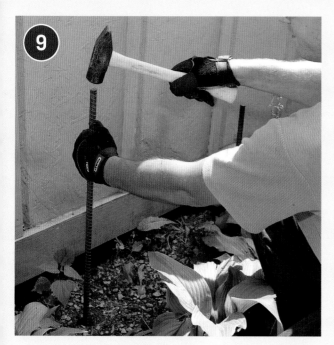

Drive a 36" length of #3 rebar (or other size that fits snugly inside the vertical support poles) into the soil at each pole impression, using a hand maul. Use a level to check the bar for plumb as you work. Drive the bars 18" into the soil.

Set stones, bricks, or other bits of masonry material around each piece of rebar. Fit the ends of the vertical support poles over the rebar so they stand squarely on the stones. Check the trellis with a level and adjust for squareness or plumb, as needed, by adding or moving the stones.

Greenhouse Companion Projects

The projects in this section all contribute to the function of a greenhouse. Some, such as planters and trellises, can be used either inside or outside the greenhouse. Others, such as the cold frame on page 178 or the Seed Starter Rack on page 198, are independent but can be used in tandem with the greenhouse to garden year-round. All of the projects will make your garden a more productive and enjoyable place to work. Keep in mind that many of these projects can be executed with materials left over from a greenhouse project. It's often wisest to start out by building the greenhouse you want, and then you can turn to the structures that best support that particular greenhouse.

In this chapter:

Cold Frame Box

An inexpensive foray into greenhouse gardening, a cold frame is practical for starting plants six to eight weeks earlier in the growing season and for hardening off seedlings. Basically, a cold frame is a box set on the ground and topped with glass or plastic. Although mechanized models with thermostatically controlled atmospheres and sashes that automatically open and close are available, you can easily build a basic cold frame yourself from materials you probably already have around the house.

The back of the frame should be about twice as tall as the front so the lid slopes to a favorable angle for capturing sunrays. Build the frame tall enough to accommodate the maximum height of the plants before they are removed. The frame can be made of brick, block, plastic, wood, or just about any material you have on hand. It should be built to keep drafts out and soil in.

If the frame is permanently sited, position it facing south to receive maximum light during winter and spring and to offer protection from wind. Partially burying it takes advantage of the insulation from the earth, but it also can cause water to collect, and the direct soil contact will shorten the lifespan of the wood frame parts. Locating your frame near a wall, rock, or building adds additional insulation and protection from the elements. Keep an inexpensive thermometer in a shaded spot inside the frame for quick reference. A bright spring day can heat a cold frame to as warm as 100 degrees Fahrenheit, so prop up or remove the cover as necessary to prevent overheating. And remember, the more you vent, the more you should water. On cold nights, especially when frost is predicted, cover the box with burlap, old quilts, or leaves to keep it warm inside.

A cold frame is positioned over tender plants early in the growing season to trap heat and moisture so they get a good, strong start. This cold frame doesn't rely on finding old windows for the top, so anyone can build it.

COLD FRAME BOX

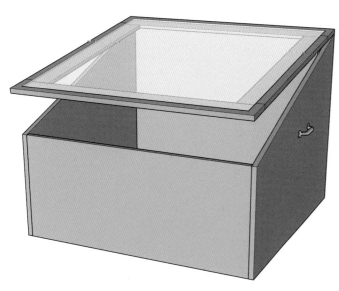

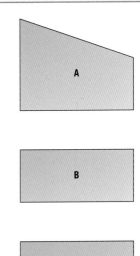

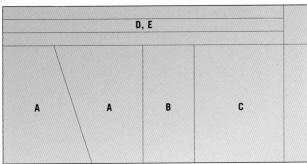

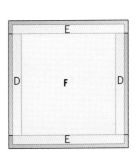

TOOLS & MATERIALS

(2) 3 × 3" butt hinges (ext.)

Exterior paint

(2) 4" utility handles

Deck screws (2" or 2½")

(4) Corner L-brackets (¾ × 2½")

#8 × ¾" wood screws

(1) ¾" × 4 × 8' plywood (ext.)

Circular saw

⅛ × 37 × 38" clear Plexiglas

Drill/driver

Exterior caulk/adhesive

Caulk gun

Pipe clamps

Exterior wood glue

Straightedge cutting guide

Eye and ear protection

Work gloves

CUTTING LIST

KEY	PART	NO.	DIMENSION	MATERIAL
A	Side	2	¾ × 16/28 × 36"	Ext. Plywood
B	Front	1	¾ × 16 × 36"	Ext. Plywood
C	Back	1	¾ × 28 × 36"	Ext. Plywood
D	Lid frame	2	¾ × 4 × 31"	Ext. Plywood
E	Lid frame	2	¾ × 4 × 38"	Ext. Plywood
F	Cover	1	⅛ × 37 × 38"	Plexiglas

How to Build a Cold Frame Box

Cut the parts. This project, as dimensioned, is designed to be made entirely from a single 4 × 8 sheet of plywood. Start by cutting the plywood lengthwise to make a 36"-wide piece.

TIP: Remove material in 4" wide strips and use the strips to make the lid frame parts and any other trim you may want to add.

Cut the parts to size with a circular saw or jigsaw and cutting guide. Mark the cutting lines first (See Diagram, previous page).

Assemble the front, back and side panels into a square box. Glue the joints and clamp them together with pipe or bar clamps. Adjust until the corners are square.

Reinforce the joints with 2 or 2½" deck screws driven through countersunk pilot holes. Drive screws every 4 to 6" along each joint.

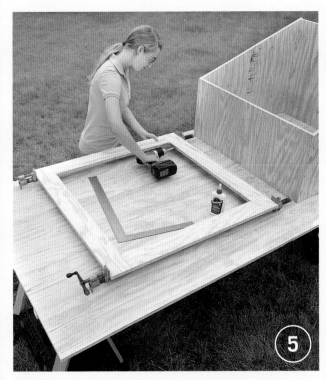

Make the lid frame. Cut the 4"-wide strips of ¾" plywood reserved from step 1 into frame parts (2 @ 31" and 2 @ 38"). Assemble the frame parts into a square 38 × 39" frame. There are many ways to join the parts so they create a flat frame. Because the Plexiglas cover will give the lid some rigidity, simply gluing the joints and reinforcing with an L-bracket at each inside corner should be more than adequate structurally.

Paint the box and the frame with exterior paint, preferably in an enamel finish. A darker color will hold more solar heat.

Lay thick beds of exterior adhesive/caulk onto the tops of the frame and then seat the Plexiglas cover into the adhesive. Clean up squeeze-out right away. Once the adhesive has set, attach the lid with butt hinges and attach the handles to the sides.

Move the cold frame to the site. Clear and level the ground where it will set if possible. Some gardeners like to excavate the site slightly.

Jumbo Cold Frame

A cold frame of any size works on the same principle as a greenhouse, capturing sunlight and heat while protecting plants from cold winds and frost. But when your planting needs outgrow a basic backyard cold frame with a window-sash roof, it makes sense to look to the greenhouse for more comprehensive design inspiration. This jumbo version offers over 17 square feet of planting area and combines the convenience of a cold frame with the full sun exposure of a greenhouse. Plus, there's ample height under the cold frame's canopy for growing taller plants.

The canopy pivots on hinges and can be propped all the way up or partially opened to several different positions for ventilating the interior to control temperature. The hinges can be separated just like door hinges (in fact, they are door hinges), so you can remove the canopy for the off season, if desired. Clear polycarbonate roofing panels make the canopy lightweight yet durable, while admitting up to 90 percent of the sun's UV rays (depending on the panels you choose).

A cold frame can extend the growing season in your garden to almost—or truly—year-round. Use an oversized cold frame like the one in this project and there may be no need to put up vegetables in the fall, because you'll have all the fresh produce you can handle.

TOOLS & MATERIALS

Circular saw or miter saw	Roofing screws with EPDM washers
Cordless drill and bits	(2) 3½" exterior-grade butt hinges with screws
Hacksaw	(2) ¼ × 4" eyebolts
Deck screws (2", 2½", 3")	3½ × 5⁄16" stainless-steel machine bolts (2 bolts with 8 washers and 2 nuts)
(5) ½" × 10' thin wall PVC pipes (the flexible type used for lawn irrigation, not schedule 40 type)	
(2) 25 × 96" corrugated polycarbonate roofing panels	(2) Heavy-duty hook-and-eye latches
30 × 24" clear acrylic panel	Outdoor thermometer with remote sensor
16" treated stakes	Work gloves
Screwdriver	Eye and ear protection

The base of the cold frame is a simple rectangle made with 2 × 6 lumber. You can pick it up and set it over an existing bed of plantings, or give it a permanent home, perhaps including a foundation of bricks or patio pavers to protect the wood from ground moisture. For additional frost protection and richer soil for your seedlings, dig down a foot or so inside the cold frame and work in a thick layer of mulch. Because all sides of the canopy have clear glazing, you don't have to worry about orienting the cold frame toward the sun; as virtually all of the interior space is equally exposed to light.

CUTTING LIST

KEY	PART	NO.	DIMENSION	MATERIAL
A	Frame side	2	1½ x 2½ x 94"	2 x 3
B	Frame end	2	1½ x 2½ x 30"	2 x 3
C	Base side	2	1½ x 5½ x 94"	2 x 6
D	Base end	2	1½ x 5½ x 30"	2 x 6
E	Frame brace	4	1½ x 2½ x 8"	2 x 3
F	Prop stick	2	¾ x 1½ x 30"	1 x 2
G	Rib	4	½ x ½ x 37"	½ PVC tubing

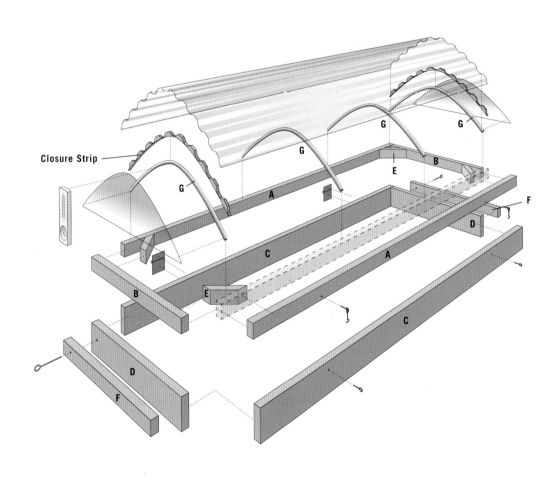

Closure Strip

How to Build a Jumbo Cold Frame

Drill pilot holes and fasten the frame end pieces between the frame side pieces with 3" deck screws to create the rectangular frame. Do the same with the base pieces to create the base. Use two screws for each joint.

Stabilize the corners of the canopy frame with braces cut to 45° angles at both ends. Install the braces on-the-flat, so their top faces are flush with the tops of the canopy frame. Drill pilot holes and fasten through the braces and into the frame with one 2½" screw at each end. Then, drive one more screw through the outside of the frame and into each end of the brace. Check the frame for square as you work.

Assemble the canopy glazing framework using ½" PVC pipe. Cut all the ribs 37" long. You can cut these easily with a miter saw, hacksaw, or jigsaw.

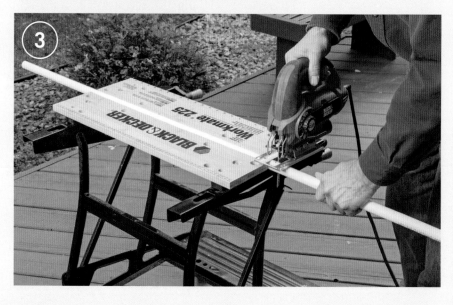

Use 2" deck screws as receptors for the PVC pipes. Drive the screws in 1" from edge and ¾" from the ends, angling the screws at about 35 to 45° toward the center. Leave about ¾" of the screw exposed. Drive two additional screws in at 32¼" from each end.

Install the PVC ribs by putting one end over the 2" screw, then curving the PVC until the other end fits over the opposite screw. Take your time with this, and use a helper if you need.

NOTE: Hopefully you've remembered to buy the flexible PVC, not the Schedule 40 type used for indoor plumbing.

Hold up and mark a smooth piece of clear acrylic for the end panels. The clear acrylic should cover the 2 × 3 and follow the curving top of the PVC. Cut the clear acrylic with a plastic-cutting jigsaw blade.

(continued)

Drill ¼" holes along the bottom of
both panels about ⅝" up from the
edge of the panel. Space the holes
2½" from ends, then every 16".
Also mark and drill rib locations on
the roof panels about 6" up from
bottom, spacing the holes at 1⅝"
and 33¼" from each end. Install the
panels 1½" up from the bottom of
the 2 × 3 with the roofing screws.
The ends of the panels should
extend 1" beyond the 2 × 3s.

Adjust the PVC ribs until the
predrilled holes in the roof panels
are centered on them, then predrill
the PVC with a ⅛" bit. Fasten the
panels to the two center ribs.

Lap the second sheet over the first,
leaving roughly the same amount
of panel hanging over the 2 × 3.
Fasten the second sheet the same
way as the first. Insert filler strips at
each end under the polycarbonate,
then drill through those into the
PVC ribs. Now add additional
screws about every ⅙". You can just
predrill the holes with the ⅛" bit
(the polycarbonate panels are soft
enough that the screws will drive
through them without cracking).

Set the clear acrylic end panels in place, butting them against the filler at the top. Mark screw locations. Place the panel on a piece of plywood and predrill with a ¼" diameter bit to avoid cracking the clear acrylic, which isn't as soft or flexible as the polycarbonate. Screw the panels in place with roofing screws, hand-tightening with a screwdriver to avoid cracking the clear acrylic. Don't overtighten.

Mount the canopy to the cold frame base with two exterior hinges. The canopy frame should fit flush over the base on all sides. Screw in two hook-and-eye latches in front.

Attach a prop stick to each side with a stainless-steel bolt and nut. Insert three washers (or more) between the prop stick and the 2 × 6 base so the prop stick clears the clear acrylic side panel. Drill a few additional ⁵⁄₁₆" holes in the stick and the frame for the eyebolts, so you can prop the canopy open at different heights. Now, prepare the ground and place the cold frame in the desired location. Anchor the base to the ground using 16" treated stakes or heavy-duty metal angles driven into the ground and secured to the frame.

Raised Planting Bed

If you live on a rural homestead with ample acreage, siting your gardens usually comes down to choosing among many good options. But if you live in a home with a smaller lot, your foray into gardening will take more planning. It will require you to make extremely efficient use of your gardening space to achieve the volume of produce you want. In many cases, this challenge is addressed by sowing your plants in raised garden beds.

Raised garden beds offer several advantages over planting at ground level. When segregated, soil can be amended in a more targeted way to support high density plantings. Also, in raised garden beds, soil doesn't suffer compaction under foot traffic or machinery, so plant roots are free to spread and breathe more easily. Vegetables and flowers planted at high densities in raised beds are placed far enough apart to avoid overcrowding but close enough to shade and choke out weeds. In raised beds, you can also water plants easily with soaker hoses, which deliver water to soil and roots rather than spraying leaves and inviting disease.

Raised garden beds can easily be customized to fit the space you have available. Just make sure you can reach the center easily. If you can only access your raised bed from one side, it's best to build it no wider than 3 feet. Beds that you can access from both sides can be as wide as 6 feet, as long as you can reach the center. You can build your raised bed as long as you'd like.

TIP: For low-growing plants, position the bed with a north-south orientation, so both sides of the bed will be exposed to direct sunlight. For taller plants, position the bed east-west.

Raised garden beds are easy to weed, simple to water, and the soil quality is easier to control, ensuring that your vegetable plants yield bountiful fresh produce. Your garden beds can be built at any height up to waist-level. It's best not to build them much taller than that, however, to make sure you can reach the center of your bed.

How to Build a Raised Planting Bed with Timbers

This basic but very sturdy raised bed is made with 4 × 4 landscape timbers stacked with their ends staggered in classic log-cabin style. The corners are pinned together with 6" galvanized spikes (or, you can use timber screws). It is lined with landscape fabric and includes several weep holes in the bottom course for drainage. Consider adding a 2 × 8 ledge on the top row (see facing page). Corner finials improve the appearance and provide hose guides to protect the plants in the bed.

Outline a 3 × 5' area with stakes and mason's string. Remove all grass inside the area, then dig a 2"-deep × 6"-wide trench along the inside perimeter of the outline. Cut each of the four timbers into one 54" piece and one 30" piece, using a reciprocating saw or circular saw.

Set the first course of timbers in the trench. Check the timbers for level along their lengths and at the corners, adding or removing soil to adjust, as needed. Position the second course on top of the first, staggering the corner joints with those in the first course. Fasten the courses together at each corner with pairs of 6" nails driven through ³⁄₁₆" pilot holes.

Line the bed with landscape fabric to contain the soil and help keep weeds out of the bed. Tack the fabric to the lower part of the top course with roofing nails. Some gardeners recommend drilling 1"-diameter weep holes in the bottom timber course at 2' intervals. Fill with a blend of soil, peat moss and fertilizer (if desired) to within 2 or 3" of the top.

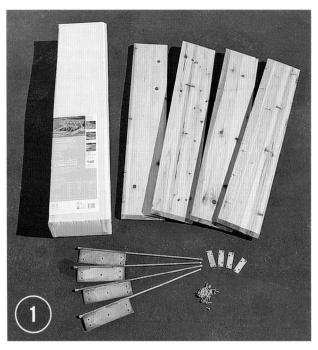

Raised garden bed kits come in many styles. Some have modular plastic or composite panels that fit together with grooves or with hardware. Others feature wood panels and metal corner hardware. Most kits can be stacked to increase bed height.

On a flat surface, assemble the panels and corner brackets (or hinge brackets) using the included hardware. Follow the kit instructions, making sure all corners are square.

Set the box down, experimenting with exact positioning until you find just the spot and angle you like. Be sure to observe the sun over an entire day when choosing the sunniest spot you can for growing vegetables. Cut around the edges of the planting bed box with a square-nose spade, move the box and then slice off the sod in the bed area.

Set the bed box onto the installation site and check it for level. Add or remove soil as needed until it is level. Stake the box to the ground with the provided hardware. Add additional box kits on top of or next to the first box. Follow the manufacturer's suggestion for connecting the modular units. Line the bed or beds with landscape fabric and fill with soil to within 2" or so of the top box.

PLANT COMPATIBILITY

VEGETABLE	LOVES	DOES NOT GET ALONG WITH	PLANTING SEASON
Asparagus	Tomatoes, parsley, basil		Early spring
Beans (bush)	Beets, carrots, cucumbers, potatoes	Fennel, garlic, onions	Spring
Cabbage & broccoli	Beets, celery, corn, dill, onions, oregano, sage	Fennel, pole beans, strawberries, tomatoes	Spring
Cantaloupe	Corn	Potatoes	Early summer
Carrots	Chives, leaf lettuce, onion, parsley, peas, rosemary, sage, tomatoes	Dill	Early spring
Celery	Beans, cabbage, cauliflower, leeks, tomatoes		Early summer
Corn	Beans, cucumbers, peas, potatoes, pumpkins, squash		Spring
Cucumbers	Beans, cabbages, corn, peas, radishes	Aromatic herbs, potatoes	Early summer
Eggplant	Beans	Potatoes	Spring
Lettuce	Carrots, cucumbers, onions, radishes, strawberries		Early spring
Onions & garlic	Beets, broccoli, cabbages, eggplant, lettuce, strawberries, tomatoes	Peas, beans	Early spring
Peas	Beans, carrots, corn, cucumbers, radishes, turnips	Chives, garlic, onions	Early spring
Potatoes	Beans, cabbage, corn, eggplant, peas	Cucumber, tomatoes, raspberries	Early spring
Pumpkins	Corn	Potatoes	Early summer
Radishes	Beans, beets, carrots, cucumbers, lettuce, peas, spinach, tomatoes		Early spring
Squash	Radishes	Potatoes	Early summer
Tomatoes	Asparagus, basil, carrots, chive, garlic, onions, parsley	Cabbages, fennel, potatoes	Dependent on the variety
Turnips	Beans, peas		Early spring

Raised Planting Bed & Cover

Raised planting beds solve a number of gardening challenges. A raised bed is much like a container garden in that it offers total control over the soil content and quality, without the worry of compaction from walking through the garden. Containment of the soil also prevents erosion, helps with weed encroachment, and improves water drainage. For many urban gardeners, a raised bed is the best—and often only—way to grow vegetables and other crop plants in tight spaces.

Another advantage of a raised bed is that the frame around the bed provides a structure for adding covers to protect plants from cold, wind, and snow, or to erect netting to keep out pests. The simple cover frame shown here is much like a hoophouse structure used by farmers to shelter rows of crops on a temporary basis. Ours is made with PVC pipe and is easy to disassemble for storage at the end of the season. The lightweight frame is perfect for a canopy of plastic sheeting (for warmth in colder weather), spun fleece (for insect protection), or deer netting (to deter deer or any other hungry critters).

The raised bed frame is made with a single course of 2 × 10 lumber. You can use smaller lumber for a shallower bed, or go higher with more courses and taller corner posts. Unless your bed will be used strictly for ornamental plants (not food), don't use pressure-treated lumber, due to the risk of chemical contamination. Instead, choose a naturally decay-resistant species such as all-heart redwood, cedar, cypress, or Douglas fir.

Filled with carefully prepared soil, a raised bed offers high yields in a relatively small space. This simple, inexpensive bed design includes wood cleats installed along its top edges—a handy feature for clamping down covers of all types.

RAISED PLANTING BED & COVER

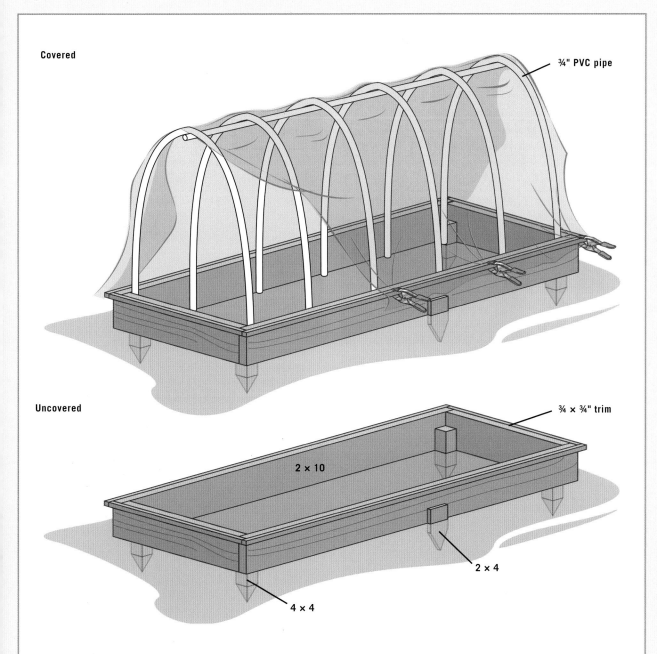

Covered

¾" PVC pipe

Uncovered

¾ × ¾" trim

2 × 10

2 × 4

4 × 4

TOOLS & MATERIALS

Tape measure

Hammer

Circular saw

Square or straightedge

Drill and countersink bit and
   ³⁄₁₆" twist bit

Reciprocating saw or handsaw

Hand sledge

Level

Permanent marker

Hacksaw or pipe cutter

Eye and ear protection

Work gloves

(2) 10' 2 × 10

(1) 8' 2 × 10

Deck screws (3½", 1¼")

(1) 8' 4 × 4

(1) 8' 2 × 4

(1) 8' 1 × 4

(7) ¾"-dia. × 10' PVC pipe

(6) 1½" #8 stainless-steel
   machine bolts and wing nuts

Cover material (8 × 14')

(12) spring clamps

How to Build a Raised Bed & Cover

Cut the two frame ends to length (45") from an 8' 2 × 10, using a circular saw and a square or straightedge to ensure straight cuts. For the frame side pieces, trim the ends of the 10' 2 × 10s, if necessary, so they are square and measure 120".

Assemble the frame by setting the sides over the ends of the end pieces so they are flush at the top and outside edges. Drill three evenly spaced pilot holes through the sides and into the end pieces and fasten the parts with 3½" deck screws.

Create the corner posts by cutting the 8' 4 × 4 into four pieces roughly 24" each. Trim the ends of each post to a point, using a reciprocating saw or handsaw.

Set the bed frame into place, then measure diagonally between opposing corners to check for square: the frame is square when the measurements are equal.

TIP: For general soil preparation, turn over the soil beneath the bed and add compost or manure, as desired, before setting down the frame.

Drive a post at each corner inside the frame, using a hand sledge and a wood block to prevent mushrooming the post top. Drive the posts until the tops are about 2" below the top of the bed frame. Check the frame for level, then drill pilot holes and fasten each side and end piece to a post with 3½" deck screws.

Add a 2 × 4 stake at the midpoint of each frame side, to help keep the lumber from bowing out over time. Cut the stake to a point and drive it down below the top edge of the frame. Tack the stake to the frame with a couple of screws.

Install the cleats: Rip a 1 × 4 into four ¾"-wide strips, using a circular saw or table saw (it's okay if the last strip isn't exactly ¾"). Fasten the strips along the perimeter of the bed frame, flush with the top edges, using 1¼" deck screws driven through pilot holes. Cut the strips to length as needed to complete each run. Fill the bed with soil and compost, as desired.

(continued)

Mark and drill the ridge pole for the cover frame, using one of the 10' PVC pipes. Make a mark 1" from each end, then mark every 24" in between. The marks should form a straight line down the length of the pipe. At each mark, drill a 3⁄16"-diameter hole straight down through the pipe.

Prepare the cover frame ribs by cutting six ¾"-diameter PVC pipes to length at 96", using a hacksaw or tubing cutter. Then, make a mark at the midpoint (48") of each rib, and drill a 3⁄16" hole straight through the pipe at each mark.

Assemble the cover frame, using 1½" machine bolts and wing nuts. Fit a rib over the top of the ridge pole at each hole location. Insert the bolt through the rib and ridge and secure with a wing nut. The wing nuts allow for quick disassembly of the frame.

ANCHOR THE FRAME

For a more secure frame that is less likely to blow away, anchor the ¾" tubing onto pieces of ½" CPVC tubing that are set into holes drilled into the raised bed walls. A ¾" bit should makes holes that are sized just right for the CPVC tubes, but drill a hole in a scrap piece first and test the fit. For extra holding power and to prevent the holes from filling with water, squeeze caulk into the hole before inserting the CPVC pipe.

Install the cover frame into the bed by fitting one end of each rib against a frame side, inside the box area, and then bending the rib and fitting the other end inside the frame. It helps to have two people for this job, starting at one end of the frame and working down.

Add the cover material of your choice. Drape the cover over the cover frame, center it side-to-side and end-to-end, and secure it on all sides with clamps fitted over the cleats. To prevent overheating with plastic covers, you can roll up the cover at the ends and clamp it to the outside ribs.

Seed Starter Rack

A seed starter rack provides a spot for you to germinate seeds and grow seedlings indoors, any time of the year (in particular, immediately before the start of the outdoor growing season). Starting your own seeds can save money over buying established plants each growing season. And in many cases, it also lets you grow less-common varieties that might not be locally available in plant form. This accessory is particularly useful if you have a modest greenhouse without supplied heating, or live in a particularly cold area with long winters.

This simple starter rack is perfect for a basement or utility room. The basic structure is built with 2 × 4s and has shelves made from ½-inch plywood. Plants that need the warmest temperatures should go on the upper shelf.

Each shelf of the rack measures 24 × 48 inches—plenty of room for four full-size seedling flats. Two fluorescent shop lights illuminate each shelf and are fully height-adjustable so you can raise or lower them as needed to provide plants with the right amounts of light and heat at different stages of development (see page 30 for tips on choosing light bulbs for your fixtures). Because seeds and seedlings can require as much as 20 hours of light per day, it's most convenient to control the lights with an automatic timer. This should be plugged into a GFCI-protected receptacle, due to all of the water used in the area. Even so, it's best to remove flats before misting or watering, to keep water away from the lights.

As with many projects in this book, you can easily modify the dimensions of the rack as shown to suit your specific needs. For a smaller unit, switch to 2-foot or 3-foot lights and resize the shelves accordingly, or make the shelves half as deep and use a single fixture for each. For a larger rack, you can make the shelves square and hang four 4-foot lights over each shelf.

This easy-to-build starter rack (left) holds up to 12 full-size seedling flats or trays and can be located practically anywhere with an accessible electrical outlet. The top shelf offers a handy space for storing extra flats and other supplies. Wire utility shelving (above) offers an easy-to-assemble alternative to building your own rack. Most inexpensive units are only 14" deep and can accommodate one row of seedling flats per shelf. Use one or two light fixtures above each shelf, as appropriate for your needs.

SEED STARTER RACK

TOOLS & MATERIALS

Circular saw

Drill/driver

Framing square

(2) 10' 2 × 4

(8) 8' 2 × 4

(1) ½" × 4 × 8' plywood

Deck screws (3½", 2½", 1⅝")

(3) 48" fluorescent light fixtures
with two 40W lamp capacity
and plug-in cord

Chain (10 linear ft.)

(6) S-hooks

Grounded power strip

Grounded automatic timer

Eye and ear protection

Work gloves

CUTTING LIST

KEY	PART	NO.	DIMENSION	MATERIAL
A	Shelf frame side	8	1½ × 3½ × 50"	2 × 4
B	Shelf frame end	8	1½ × 3½ × 21"	2 × 4
C	Leg	4	1½ × 3½ × 79½"	2 × 4
D	Shelf	4	½ × 24 × 48"	Plywood

48" fluorescent light fixture–
1 per shelf

Timer in wall receptacle

How to Build a Seed Starter Rack

Cut all of the wood parts for the shelf frames, using a circular saw or power miter saw. Cut one shelf frame side and two shelf frame ends from each of four 8' 2 × 4s, and cut the remaining four shelf frame sides from two 10' 2 × 4s. Cut each of the four legs from an 8' 2 × 4.

Assemble the shelf frames with 3½" deck screws. Position the side pieces of each frame over the ends of the end pieces and so their top edges are flush. Drill pilot holes and drive two screws through the sides and into the ends. Complete all four shelf frames using the same technique.

Add the shelves. Cut four shelves at 24 × 48", using a circular saw and straightedge cutting guide. Check each shelf frame with a framing square, then lay the shelf over the top so it's centered side-to-side and end-to-end. Fasten the shelf to the frame with 1⅝" deck screws.

Mark the shelf locations onto the legs. Measuring from the bottom of one leg, make marks at 7½", 31½", and 55½". These marks represent the top edges of the shelves; the top shelf is installed flush with the top ends of the legs. Use the framing square to transfer the layout marks to the remaining three legs.

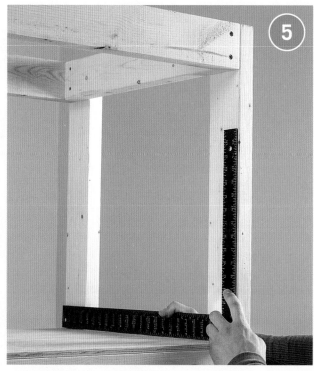

Fasten the shelves to each leg with two 2½" deck screws driven through the shelf ends and into the legs. The top edges of each shelf should be on its layout marks (or flush with the ends of the legs), and the front and rear sides should be flush with the outside edges of the legs. Use a square to make sure the shelf and legs are perpendicular before fastening.

Hang the light fixtures, using chain and S-hooks. Cut the chain into 18" lengths, using wire cutters, and attach each to one end of each fixture, using S-hooks or wire, as applicable. Attach the other end of the chains to the plywood shelf above, using S-hooks.

Route the fixture cords to the nearest leg of the rack and secure them with zip ties or insulated cable staples. Be sure to leave enough slack in the cord to allow for moving the fixture up and down. If necessary, use an approved extension cord to extend a fixture cord to the power strip location.

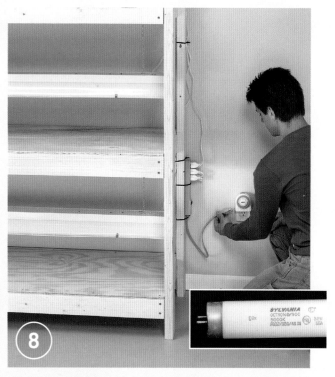

Plug the light fixtures into an approved (grounded) power strip, and plug the power strip into a 24-hour timer installed in a GFCI-protected wall receptacle. If the circuit or receptacle is not GFCI-protected, replace the existing receptacle with a GFCI receptacle, following the manufacturer's directions.

Greenhouse Workbench

Good, sturdy worktables are indispensable tools for most greenhouse gardeners. That's why almost any sizable greenhouse is furnished with some kind of workbench running down both long sides of the building. Benches hold plants at a comfortable level, saving your back and your knees during those many hours of tending and watering. They also make for healthier plants, keeping them above the cooler air near the floor and, with permeable bench tops, allowing airflow and even some light to reach them from below.

In this project, you'll learn how to build a basic, easily adaptable worktable, to which you can add the top and shelf surfaces of your choice. Made with 2 × 4

lumber, the bench frame is simple, inexpensive, and durable. And because it's put together with screws, you can easily disassemble the main parts for compact off-season storage (a great feature for temporary hoophouse gardeners). Several good options for top and shelf surfaces are shown on page 205.

Regarding adaptability, you might want to change the dimensions of the bench as shown to suit your needs and/or fit the available space in your greenhouse. Simply add or subtract whatever you need to modify the bench width, length, or height. You can also add a second shelf to double the storage space for seedling flats and other short items, or to keep garden tools conveniently close to the bench top.

A greenhouse bench should be practical, lightweight, and space-efficient. This simple bench is highly adaptable and easy to move around. The ample lower shelf provides maximum storage area without taking up unnecessary floor space.

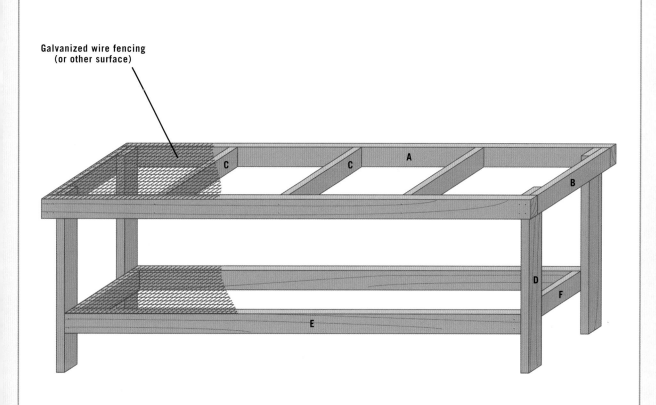

Galvanized wire fencing
(or other surface)

TOOLS & MATERIALS

Tape measure

Hammer

Circular saw or power miter saw

Clamps

Drill/driver

Framing square

Aviation snips

Metal file

(8) 8' cedar or PT 2 × 4

Deck screws (2½", 3½")

24"-wide steel mesh
(or other tabletop material)

1½" galvanized horseshoe nails

Eye and ear protection

Work gloves

CUTTING LIST

KEY	PART	NO.	DIMENSION	MATERIAL
A	Top frame side	2	1½ × 3½ × 96"	2 × 4
B	Top frame end	2	1½ × 3½ × 22"	2 × 4
C	Top supports	3	1½ × 3½ × 22"	2 × 4
D	Leg	4	1½ × 3½ × 32"	2 × 4
E	Shelf frame side	2	1½ × 3½ × 90"	2 × 4
F	Shelf frame end	2	1½ × 3½ × 19"	2 × 4

How to Build a Greenhouse Workbench

Assemble the top frame by clamping the side pieces over the ends of the end pieces so they're flush along the top edges. Drill pilot holes and fasten each corner with two 3½" deck screws.

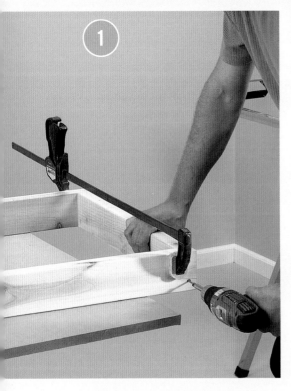

Install the top supports between the side pieces, spacing them 24" apart on center. First, mark layout lines onto both side pieces, then square the frame by measuring diagonally between opposing corners; the frame is square when the measurements are equal. Fasten the supports with pairs of 3½" deck screws.

Attach the legs to the inside corners of the top frame, using 2½" deck screws. The top ends of the legs should be flush with the top edges of the frame. Use a framing square to make sure each leg is perpendicular to the frame before fastening.

Assemble the shelf frame in the same manner as the top frame. Mark the inside face of each leg 10" up from the bottom end. Position the shelf frame with its top edges on the marks, and fasten it to the legs with 2½" deck screws driven through the frame ends. The side frame pieces should be flush with the outside edges of the legs.

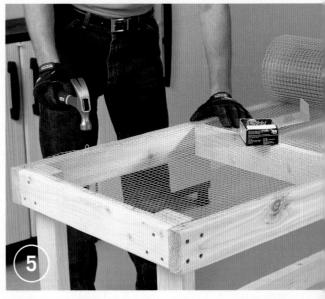

Add the top and shelf surface material. Galvanized wire mesh fencing is shown here (see next page for other options). Cut the 24"-tall fencing to length at 95", using aviation snips. Round over any sharp cut ends of wire with a metal file. Center the mesh over the top frame, leaving a ½" margin at all sides. Fasten the mesh with 1½" horseshoe nails. Trim and install the shelf mesh in the same fashion.

Options for Bench Top & Shelf Surfaces

Expanded steel mesh is stiffer and has smaller holes than metal wire fencing, offering a more solid surface while maintaining permeability. Fasten steel mesh to the frame parts with heavy-duty staples or horseshoe nails. Do not use stucco lath, which has a rough surface and sharp steel edges.

Exterior plywood offers a smooth, continuous surface for a bench top or shelf. One full 4 × 8' sheet of ¾"-thick plywood will cover a full-size bench top and shelf. Fasten plywood to the frame parts with 1½" deck screws. Keep in mind that a plywood surface won't drain like a permeable material; you may want to pitch the bench slightly to one side for drainage. Coat it with deck stain or paint to make it easier to clean and more stain resistant.

1 × 4 or 1 × 6 cedar boards or decking boards make an attractive top surface and offer some runoff, depending on how widely the boards are gapped. For the bench top, run boards parallel to the length of the top frame; for the shelf, run them perpendicular to the length of the shelf frame.

Protect stored items from draining water with a simple "roof" made with a single panel of corrugated plastic or fiberglass roofing. Use 2 × 4s between the leg pairs to support the panel, sloping the panel down toward one end at ¼" per foot. Secure the panel at the top end with a couple of screws.

Built-In Potting Bench

Any greenhouse of reasonable size and structural integrity is a candidate for a useful and beautiful built-in workbench. A bench like the one in this project is a streamlined greenhouse addition that makes best use of the least amount of materials and fits in seamlessly with the greenhouse interior. It can also be easily adapted to different gardeners—made lower or higher, longer, or deeper as need dictates. That makes it much more valuable than any prefab potting bench you can buy. The design includes a handy lower shelf to keep potting materials off the greenhouse floor and a wonderful compartment beneath removable slats where you can blend your own batches of potting mix.

This built-in bench is made of standard construction grade 2 × 4s and pressure-treated 1 × 6 deck boards. Because it is covered by a roof, leaving the bench unpainted will not materially affect its longevity. But greenhouses and gardening sheds usually aren't simple utility areas. Investing a little time and money in painting the bench is well worth it (technically, the potting bench seen here is coated with semi-transparent deck stain).

This potting bench uses the structural members of a greenhouse kneewall for support. The five slats at the right end can be removed to access a shelf for buckets and planters.

BUILT-IN POTTING BENCH

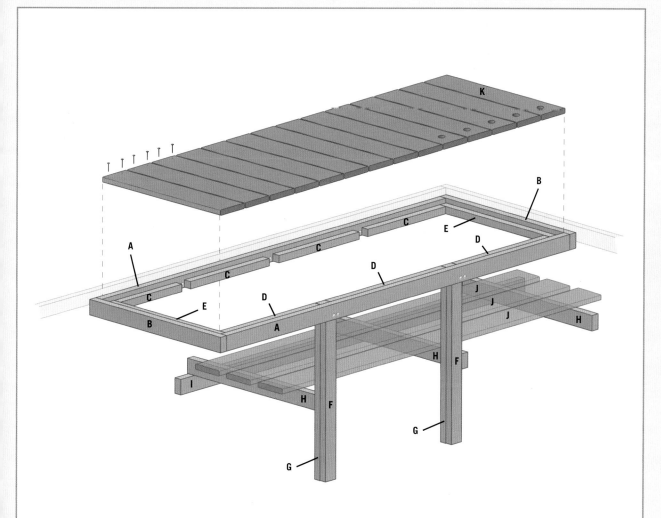

TOOLS & MATERIALS

Tape measure
Deck screws (2½", 3")
Lag screws (⅜ × 3")
Carriage bolts (½ × 3½")
Level
Exterior-rated wood glue
Drill/driver
Circular saw or power miter saw
Clamps
(6) 2 × 4" × 8'
(3) 2 × 2" × 8'
Eye and ear protection

CUTTING LIST

KEY	PART	NO.	DIMENSION	MATERIAL
A	Front/back frame	2	1½ × 3½ × 81"	2 × 4
B	Frame ends	2	1½ × 3½ × 22"	2 × 4
C	Cleats-back	4	1½ × 1½ × 16"	2 × 2
D	Cleats-front	3	1½ × 1½ × 22"	2 × 2
E	Cleats-side	2	1½ × 1½ × 19"	2 × 2
F	Leg half	2	1½ × 3½ × 31½"	2 × 4
G	Leg half	2	1½ × 3½ × 33½"	2 × 4
H	Shelf support	3	1½ × 3½ × 20½"	2 × 4
I	Back wall ledger	1	1½ × 3½ × 32"	2 × 4
J	Shelf board	3	4/4 × 5½ × 60"	Deckboard
K	Top slat	14	4/4 × 5½ × 18½"	Deckboard

How to Build a Built-In Potting Bench

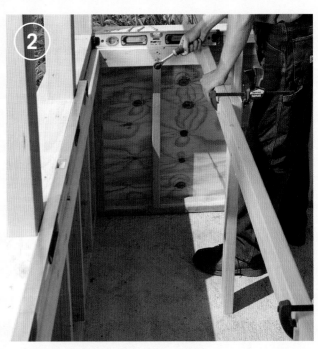

Pre-assemble the frame that is the benchtop support. Cut the 2 × 4 front, back, and ends to length and then join them with 3" deck screws and exterior-rated wood glue.

Attach the benchtop frame to the greenhouse wall studs using ⅜ × 3" lag screws. Before driving the lag screws, tack the back of the frame to the long wall with deck screws. The tops should be 36" above the floor. Then, clamp a 2 × 4 brace to the front rail of the frame and adjust it until level. Drill guide holes and drive one lag screw per wall stud at the back rail and on the ends.

Install the front legs. Each leg is created with a pair of 2 × 4s face-nailed or screwed together. The front 2 × 4 in each pair should fit between the frame and the floor. The back 2 × 4 in each pair is 2½" longer to provide a surface for attaching the frame and legs. Join the leg halves with glue and 2½" deck screws.

Attach each leg to the frame with a pair of ½ × 3½" carriage bolts. Drill guide holes for the bolt and counterbores for the nuts and washers in the back face of the frame. Do not use washers behind carriage bolt heads.

Attach a 2 × 4 ledger to the front wall studs to support the 2 × 4 shelf supports that run from the front of the bench to the wall. Use 3" deck screws driven at kneewall stud locations.

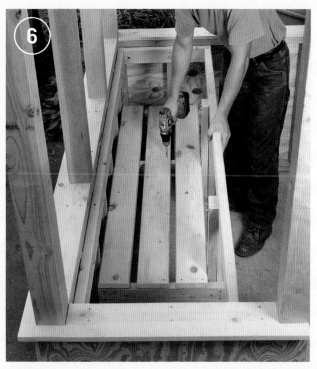

Attach 2 × 4 shelf supports to the legs and attach a 2 × 4 shelf support to the endwall. Then, fasten the shelving material to the tops of the supports. The best height for the shelf depends on the height of the containers you plan to set on the shelves beneath the removable section of the top.

Glue and screw 2 × 2 cleats around the inside perimeter of the benchtop frame. The cleats should be positioned so they are level and the top faces of the deckboard slats will be about ⅛" above the frame tops when they rest on the cleats. Install a full-length cleat along the back wall and fill in between the legs at the front.

Cut the benchtop slats from treated or cedar decking (or composite if you prefer). Attach the slats over the first two bays by driving a pair of deck screws into each slat end and the cleat below. Do not fasten the deckboards over the right end bay. Drill 1" finger holes near the end of each board and simply set them on the cleats so they can be removed to access the shelf below. If you wish, coat the bench with deck finish.

Simple Potting Bench

A multi-functional workstation, like the High-Low Potting Bench on pages 214 to 217, offers great versatility that makes it useful in just about any greenhouse. But sometimes, all you really want from your work area is a big, broad surface with plenty of room to spread out and get busy. This workhorse of a bench is modeled after the most-used workspace in any home: the kitchen countertop. At 36 inches tall, the bench is the same height as most kitchen counters, and at 28 inches wide, it's slightly deeper than standard countertops—but not so deep that you can't easily reach across to the other side. The symmetrical configuration allows you to push any part of the bench against a greenhouse wall and still get plenty of light penetration.

There's also no need to worry about a moisture-laden greenhouse environment. The understructure is made with moisture-resistant, pressure-treated lumber, and the top is made up of composite decking boards that won't split, rot, or splinter and require no protective finish.

Of course, if you've always wished your kitchen counters were a bit higher or lower, you can simply add or subtract a few inches from the given dimension for the bench legs. You can also change the length of the bench to fit a small greenhouse, if necessary. Shortening the whole thing by 2 feet allows you to build it with standard 8-foot lumber and decking instead of 12-foot and 10-foot pieces.

This potting bench has a 28 × 71" top and is built with four 2 × 4s and three standard-size decking boards. The handy pot shelf below the bench top is made with a cutoff from one of the deck boards.

SIMPLE POTTING BENCH

¾" overhang all sides

TOOLS & MATERIALS

Tape measure

Circular saw

Drill

Piloting-countersink bit

Framing square

Clamps

(3) 12' pressure-treated 2 × 4s

Deck screws (2½", 3½")

(1) 10' pressure-treated 2 × 4

(3) 12' 1 × 6 composite decking boards

Sandpaper

Eye and ear protection

Work gloves

CUTTING LIST

KEY	PART	NO.	DIMENSION	MATERIAL
A	Top frame side	2	1½ × 3½ × 69½"	2 × 4
B	Top frame end	2	1½ × 3½ × 23½"	2 × 4
C	Top supports	4	1½ × 3½ × 23½"	2 × 4
D	Leg	4	1½ × 3½ × 35"	2 × 4
E	Leg support	2	1½ × 3½ × 16½" (field measure)	2 × 4
F	Stretcher	1	1½ × 3½ × 63½" (field measure)	2 × 4
G	Top decking	5	1 × 5½ × 71"	1 × 6 decking
H	Pot shelf	1	1 × 5½ × 68"	1 × 6 decking

How to Build a Simple Potting Bench

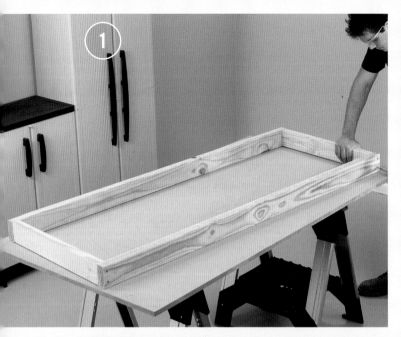

Cut the two top frame sides from one 12' 2 × 4, using a circular saw or power miter saw. Cut the two top frame ends and the four top supports from another 12' 2 × 4. Fit the side pieces over the ends of the end pieces so all top edges are flush. Drill countersunk pilot holes and fasten the pieces together with two 3½" deck screws at each joint.

Mark the layout for the top supports. Measuring from one end of the top frame, mark both frame sides every 13⅜". Check the top frame for square, using a framing square. Install the top supports between the frame sides with 3½" deck screws driven through the frame sides and into the supports. Make sure the supports and frame sides are flush across the top.

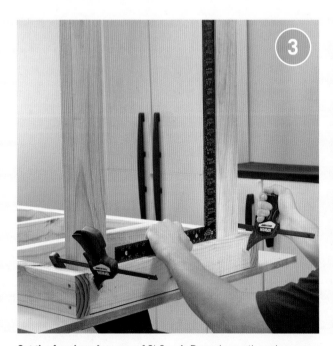

Cut the four legs from one 12' 2 × 4. Round-over the edges on the bottom end of each leg, using sandpaper, a file, or a router and roundover bit; this prevents splintering if the table is slid around. Install the legs at the inside corners of the top frame, driving 2½" deck screws through the legs and into the top frame ends. Also screw through the top frame sides and into the legs. Make sure the legs are square to the frame before fastening.

Mark the inside edge of each leg, 10" up from its bottom end. Measure the distance between each leg pair and cut a leg support to fit snugly between the legs, using the 10' 2 × 4. Install the leg supports with their bottom edges on the marks; drive 3½" screws toenail style through the top and bottom edges of the supports and into the legs.

Cut the 2 × 4 stretcher to fit snugly between the leg supports, using the remainder of the 10' 2 × 4. Install the stretcher so it's centered side-to-side on each support, with the top edges flush. Drive 3½" screws through the outsides of the leg supports and into the stretcher ends.

Cut the top decking boards to length. Clamp the first board in place so it overhangs the front and ends of the top frame by ¾". If the deck boards are crowned (slightly curved across the face), make sure the convex side faces up. Drill two pilot holes at the center of each top frame end and top support location, countersinking the holes slightly. Fasten the board with 2½" deck screws.

Install the remaining deck boards so all of their ends are perfectly aligned and each board is gapped ⅛" from the next (without gaps, the joints would trap dirt). Use pieces of ⅛"-thick hardboard or two ⅛"-diameter drill bits to set the gaps. The last board should overhang the rear frame side by ¾".

Complete the pot shelf by cutting the remaining half-piece of deck board to length. Position the board so it is centered side-to-side over the stretcher and overhangs both leg supports by ¾". Fasten the board to the stretcher and leg supports with 2½" deck screws driven through pilot holes.

High-Low Potting Bench

A workbench like this can be absolutely ideal against the back (north) wall of a greenhouse. It actually combines two work benches in one: a regular waist-level bench to fill seed trays or pots and a longer, lower bench that can hold supplies or plants while still allowing a maximum of sunlight to reflect back and penetrate deeply into the greenhouse. As a plus, it's constructed of materials that are ideal for the moisture-heavy environment and temperature fluctuations common to any greenhouse.

What makes this potting bench different from most other potting benches is that the work surfaces are at appropriate heights for gardening tasks. The work surface is 30 inches high, making it easier to reach down into pots. The low work surface is just over a foot high, so you won't have to lift heavy objects such as large pots or bags of soil. In addition to the high-low work surfaces, this bench also features a shelf and hook rail to keep small supplies and tools within reach, yet still off the main work area.

A potting bench gets wet and it gets dirty, so rot- and moisture-resistant materials were chosen to build this bench. The frame is made with pressure-treated pine lumber, and the work surfaces are composite deck boards. The composite material provides a smooth surface that will not splinter and is easy to clean.

TOOLS & MATERIALS

Tape measure	Bandsaw or jigsaw	(4) 2 × 4" × 8' pine
Cup hooks	Work gloves	(1) 1¼ × 5½" × 6' pine
Clamps	Eye and ear protection	(4) ⅝" × 8' deck boards
Sandpaper	(1) 1 × 2" × 8' pine	Exterior-rated screws (1¼", 2", 2½")
Drill	(2) 1 × 4" × 8' pine	Solid-color exterior paint or stain

Not all pots are the same height. With two different working heights, this bench is comfortable to use whether you're planting seeds in starter trays or planting a 5-gallon planter with tomatoes.

HIGH-LOW POTTING BENCH

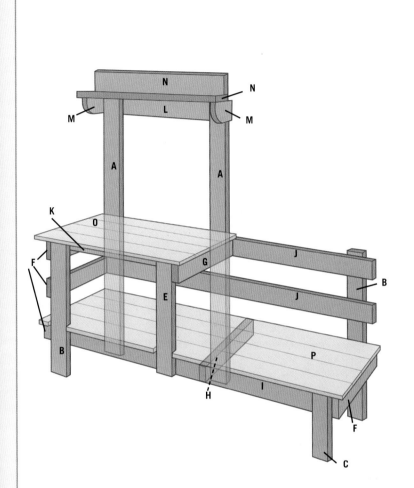

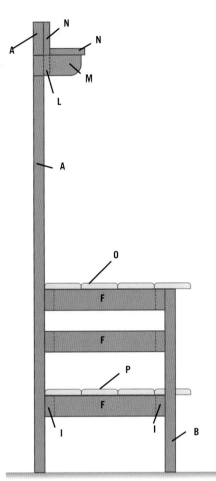

CUTTING LIST

KEY	PART	NO.	DIMENSION	MATERIAL
A	Long leg	2	1½ × 3½ × 62¾"	Treated pine
B	Mid-length leg	2	1½ × 3½ × 29"	Treated pine
C	Short leg	1	1½ × 3½ × 12"	Treated pine
D	Back strut*	1	1½ × 3½ × 54¼"	Treated pine
E	Front strut	1	1½ × 3½ × 20½"	Treated pine
F	Outside cross supports	4	¾ × 3½ × 22"	Treated pine
G	Middle top cross support	1	1½ × 3½ × 19¾"	Treated pine
H	Middle bottom cross support	1	1½ × 3½ × 16"	Treated pine

KEY	PART	NO.	DIMENSION	MATERIAL
I	Bottom rails	2	1½ × 3½ × 60"	Treated pine
J	Back rails	2	¾ × 3½ × 60"	Treated pine
K	Front rail	1	¾ × 1½ × 30"	Treated pine
L	Hook rail	1	¾ × 3½ × 30"	Treated pine
M	Shelf supports	2	¾ × 3½ × 7"	Treated pine
N	Shelf/shelf back	2	1¼ × 5½ × 31½"	Treated pine
O	High worktop	4	1¼ × 5½ × 33½"	Deck boards
P	Low worktop	4	1¼ × 5½ × 62½"	Deck boards

*Not shown

How to Build a High-Low Potting Bench

Cut the Frame Parts

Cut all of the frame and shelf parts to length. Draw a 3½-inch radius on the front bottom corner of each shelf support. Cut along the radius lines with a jigsaw or bandsaw (photo 1). Sand the profiles smooth. Apply a solid-color exterior deck and siding stain to all sides of the frame and shelf parts. Staining these parts isn't mandatory, but it's an opportunity to customize your workbench, and the stain will extend the life of the parts.

Assemble the Frame

Attach two back rails and one bottom rail to the long leg, back strut, and back right mid-length leg with 2-inch deck screws. Check that all of the parts intersect at 90-degree angles. Attach the front rail and one bottom rail to the left front mid-length leg, front strut, and short leg. Connect the back assembly and front assembly by attaching them to the cross supports (photo 2).

Cut the shelf supports. Use a bandsaw or a jigsaw to make the 3½" radius roundovers on the ends of the shelf supports. Sand smooth.

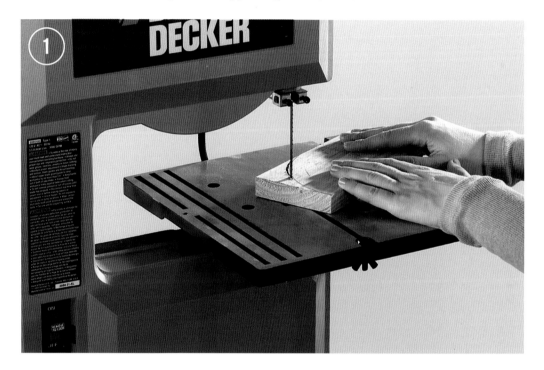

Assemble the bench frame. Clamp the cross supports to the front and back assemblies. Attach the cross supports with 2" deck screws.

Attach the Worktop Planks

Cut the deck boards that will be used to create the work surfaces to length. We used composite deck boards because they require little maintenance and are easy to clean. Place the front deck board for the lower work surface against the backside of the front left leg and front strut. Mark the point where the front leg and strut intersect the deck board. Using these marks, draw the 3¾" deep notch outlines and cut out the notches with a jigsaw (photo 3).

Place the top and bottom deck boards on the cross supports, leaving a ¼-inch space between the boards. Drill two pilot holes that are centered over the cross supports in each deck board. Attach the deck boards with 2-inch deck screws (photo 4). If you are using composite deck boards, use specially designed decking screws.

Attach the Shelf & Rack

Attach the shelf back, shelf hook rail, and shelf supports to the long leg and back strut with 2½-inch deck screws. Attach the shelf to the shelf supports with 2-inch deck screws. Fasten the hooks to the shelf hook rail (photo 5).

Cut notches. Lay out notches in the front board for the low work surface where the board must fit around the front leg and front strut. Use a jigsaw to cut the notches.

Install the worktop slats. Use composite screws to attach the composite deck boards that create the upper and lower worktops.

Install the shelf and hook rail. Attach the shelf to the shelf supports. Drill pilot holes for each screw to prevent splitting the shelf supports. Once the hook rail is installed twist in the cup hooks.

Lettuce Table

The lettuce table solves a number of gardening problems that home gardeners confront when growing tasty vegetables and herbs. First, and most important, it moves the crop up and out of the way of rabbits, slugs, and other destructive pests. Second, it's portable, so it can be moved to follow or avoid the sun, or brought into the garage on frosty nights. Third, it can be set up on convenient but barren spots like decks, patios, and driveways. Fourth, it allows you to garden at a comfortable height, saving wear and tear on knees and backs. Fifth, you can easily replace the growing media every year and precisely control moisture and fertilizer, giving you better, more predictable yields. And finally, it provides accessible gardening for those in wheelchairs.

The frame of this lettuce table, which will be in contact with the soil, can be made from cedar, redwood, or any other naturally rot-resistant wood. It is left unfinished on the inside. Pressure-treated wood is used for the rest of the framework because it's less expensive and will resist decay for decades. The galvanized hardware cloth across the bottom is an inexpensive way to support the weight of the soil; you can substitute cedar boards, galvanized metal flashing, or any other rot-resistant, nontoxic material that can hold the weight. No matter what you use to hold the weight, the soil is held in place with heavy-duty landscape fabric or aluminum screen mesh.

The lettuce table can be used to grow more than lettuce. It simply draws its name from its original purpose, which is to provide a shallow bed for growing lettuces in an easy-to-reach spot that can be moved easily around your yard. This interpretation is on the large side to allow you to grow several varieties, but you can easily modify the simple plan to build a more compact version.

TOOLS & MATERIALS

2 × 4" × 8' cedar (1)

2 × 4" × 12' cedar (1)

2 × 4" × 8' pressure-treated (1)

2 × 4" × 12' pressure-treated (3)

1 × 2" × 8' pressure-treated (3)

¼" galvanized hardware cloth

Stapler with 5/16" stainless steel staples

Landscape fabric

Construction adhesive

2½" deck screws (1 lb.)

Countersink bit

Framing square

Leather gloves

Drill

Miter saw

Tin snips

Hammer

Caulk gun

Clamps

CUTTING LIST

PART	NO.	DIMENSION	MATERIAL
Tray side	2	2 × 4 × 72"	Cedar
Tray ends and divider	3	2 × 4 × 21"	Cedar
Outer leg	4	2 × 4 × 36"	Pressure-treated
Inner leg	4	2 × 4 × 20½"	Pressure-treated
Bottom leg	4	2 × 4 × 8½"	Pressure-treated
Stretcher	1	2 × 4 × 69"	Pressure-treated
Top stretcher	1	2 × 4 × 72"	Pressure-treated
Center support	1	2 × 4 × 19"	Pressure-treated
Side rail	2	2 × 4 × 24"	Pressure-treated
Side trim	2	1 × 2 × 71"	Pressure-treated
End trim	2	1 × 2 × 17"	Pressure-treated

How to Build a Lettuce Table

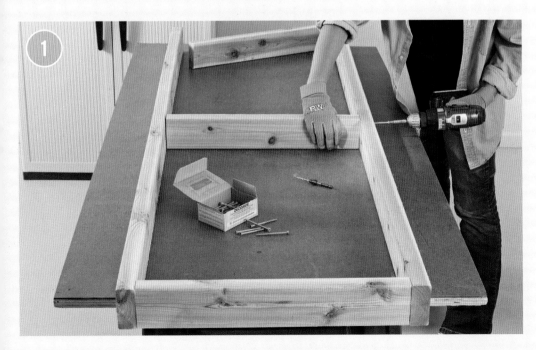

Cut the parts for the table frame to length and assemble the cedar top tray with the center divider. Predrill all screw holes to avoid splits, and use two screws at each corner. Use 2½" (or 3") deck screws. This design is for a 2 × 6 ft. tray, but you can make it larger or smaller.

(continued)

Wearing leather gloves, cut the hardware cloth to size. Cut out a 2 × 4" section at each corner for the legs. Center it on the underside of the cedar frame—it should be about ¼" in from the edge on all sides. Nail it every 6" on the center divider, but first mark and cut out a 2 × 4" slot at the center of the divider. Pull the cloth flat and nail it several times on each side and the ends. No need to overdo it—the edges of the cloth will be covered and secured with 1 × 2s later.

Cut the legs from the pressure-treated wood and assemble them into two leg pairs. Screw the inner and outer legs together, leaving a 3½" gap at the top. The top frame will sit on the ledges created at the top. Leave the bottom legs off for now. Make sure the legs are parallel to each other, then join them together with the side rails. Spread a bead of construction adhesive before attaching the two pieces. Set the legs down parallel to each other and join them with the side rails.

With the tray turned upside down, fit the legs onto the ends. Check that they're square to the frame and sitting flat underneath it—if you see daylight between the inner leg and the tray, trim the outer leg a little so the gap disappears. Screw each leg to both parts of the cedar frame.

Attach the stretcher with 2½" screws. Use clamps to hold the wood in place while you predrill and fasten. Also measure and cut the bottoms of the legs, and fasten with adhesive and screws.

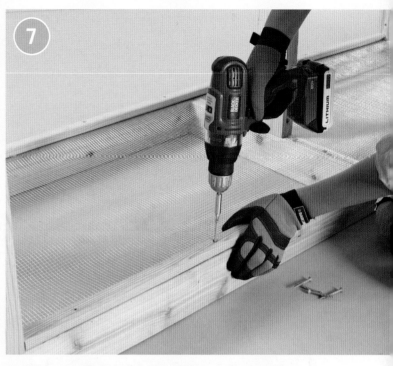

Place the tray on the ground, right-side up. Screw the top stretcher to the rails and lower stretcher. Measure the distance from the stretchers to the center divider and cut and fasten the support. Add ⅟₁₆" to your measurement just to make sure you have a snug fit.

Predrill the 1 × 2s every 8 to 10". Flip the tray over then screw the 1 × 2s to the bottom of the tray, flush with the outside edges and covering the hardware cloth.

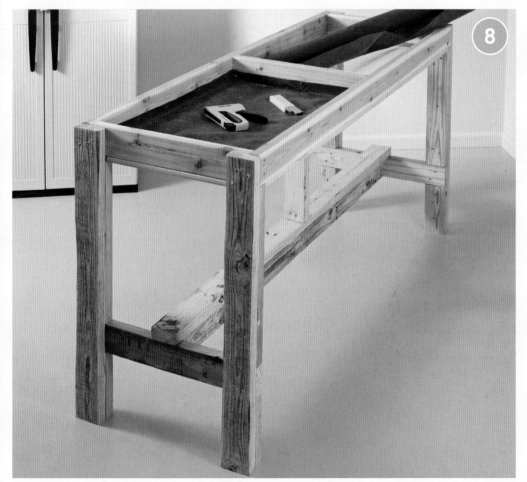

Finally, staple on landscape fabric or aluminum screen on the inside of the tray to hold the soil in. Fill the tray with a soilless growing media and fertilizer—not ordinary topsoil. For best results, replace the soilless mix every year, as it becomes compressed over time.

Trellis Planter

This simple, very stable planter-and-trellis combo exploits the durable nature of cedar to create a greenhouse feature ideally suited to the rigors, sun exposure, and moisture ever present in any greenhouse structure. The design showcases the wood in an incredibly useful greenhouse planter perfect for training edibles to grow vertically.

Because the 2 × 2 lattice trellis is attached to the planter, not permanently fastened to a wall or railing, it can be moved easily to follow changing sunlight patterns within the greenhouse or even shuttled outside in warmer months to make room for other plants or just to give the planter's occupants some outside exposure. You may even want to consider installing wheels or casters on the base for greater mobility.

Building the trellis planter is a very simple job. The trellis portion is made entirely of strips of 2 × 2 cedar, fashioned together in a crosshatch pattern. The planter bin is a basic wood box, with panel sides and a two-board bottom with drainage holes that rests on a scalloped base. The trellis is screwed permanently to the back of the planter bin.

All manner of plants can be grown vertically in a greenhouse environment, including some surprising candidates, such as tomatoes, zucchini, and even miniature melon varieties. By training edibles that normally sprawl to climb up the more orderly surface of a trellis like this, you'll free up room in your greenhouse, make it easier to tend the growing plants, and increase airflow—preventing disease in the process.

TOOLS & MATERIALS

(1) 2 × 6" × 8' cedar	1"-dia. spade bit	Circular saw
(1) 2 × 4" × 6' cedar	Counterbore bit	Miter saw
(4) 2 × 2" × 8' cedar	Jigsaw	Finishing materials
(3) 1 × 6" × 8' cedar	Compass	Eye and ear protection
(1) 1 × 2" × 6' cedar	Square	Work gloves
Tape measure	Moisture-resistant glue	
Drill	Deck screws (1⅝", 2½")	

TRELLIS PLANTER

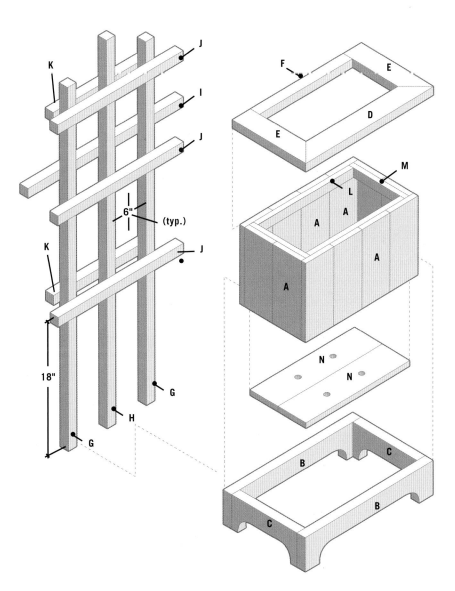

Overall Size:
69" High
17¼" Deep
30" Long

6" (typ.)

18"

CUTTING LIST

KEY	PART	NO.	DIMENSION	MATERIAL
A	Box slats	12	⅞ × 5½ × 13"	Cedar
B	Base front and back	2	1½ × 5½ × 25"	Cedar
C	Base ends	2	1½ × 5½ × 12¾"	Cedar
D	Cap front	1	1½ × 3½ × 25"	Cedar
E	Cap ends	2	1½ × 3½ × 14¼"	Cedar
F	Cap back	1	1½ × 1½ × 18"	Cedar
G	End posts	2	1½ × 1½ × 59½"	Cedar

KEY	PART	NO.	DIMENSION	MATERIAL
H	Center post	1	1½ × 1½ × 63½"	Cedar
I	Long rail	1	1½ × 1½ × 30"	Cedar
J	Medium rails	3	1½ × 1½ × 24"	Cedar
K	Short rails	2	1½ × 1½ × 18"	Cedar
L	Long cleats	2	⅞ × 1½ × 18½"	Cedar
M	Short cleats	2	⅞ × 1½ × 11"	Cedar
N	Bottom boards	2	⅞ × 5½ × 20¼"	Cedar

How to Build a Trellis Planter

Step 1: Build the Planter Bin

1. Cut the box slats (A) and cleats (L, M) to length. Arrange the slats edge-to-edge in two groups of four and two groups of two, with tops and bottoms flush.

2. Center a long cleat (L) at the top of each set of four slats, so the distance from each end of the cleat to the end of the panel is the same. Attach the cleats to the four-slat panels by driving 1⅝" deck screws (photo 1) through the cleats and into the slats.

3. Lay the short cleats (M) at the tops of the two-slat panels. Attach them to the slats the same way.

4. Arrange all four panels into a box shape and apply moisture-resistant wood glue to the joints. Attach the panels by driving 1⅝" deck screws through the four-slat panels and into the ends of the two-slat panels.

Step 2: Install the Bin Bottom

1. Cut the bottom boards (N) to length. Set the bin upside down on your work surface, and mark reference lines on the inside faces of the panels, ⅞" in from the bottom of the bin. Insert the bottom boards into the bin, aligned with the reference lines to create a ⅞" recess. Scraps of 1× cedar can be put beneath the bottom boards as spacers.

2. Drill ⅛" pilot holes through the panels. Counterbore the holes slightly with a counterbore bit. Fasten the bottom boards by driving 1⅝" deck screws through the panels and into the edges and ends of the bottom boards.

Step 3: Build the Planter Base

1. The planter base is scalloped to create feet at the corners.

2. Cut the base front and back (B) and the base ends (C) to length. To draw the contours for the scallops on the front and back boards, set the point of a compass at the bottom edge of the base front, 5" in from one end. Set the compass to a 2½" radius and draw a curve to mark the curved end of the cutout. Draw a straight line to connect the tops of the curves, 2½" up from the bottom of the board, to complete the scalloped cutout.

3. Make the cutout with a jigsaw, then sand any rough spots. Use the board as a template for marking a matching cutout on the base back.

4. Draw a similar cutout on one base end, except with the point of the compass 3½" in from the ends. Cut out both end pieces with a jigsaw.

5. Draw reference lines for wood screws ¾" from the ends of the base front and back. Drill three evenly spaced pilot holes through the lines. Counterbore the holes. Fasten the base ends between the base front and back by driving three evenly spaced deck screws at each joint.

Attach the side cleats flush with the tops of the side boards.

The recess beneath the bottom boards in the planter bin provides access for driving screws.

Before attaching the cap ends, drill pilot holes through the mitered ends of the cap-front ends.

Step 4: Attach the Bin to the Base

1. Set the base frame and planter bin on their backs. Position the planter bin inside the base so it extends ⅞" past the top of the base.

2. Drive 1⅝" deck screws through the planter bin and into the base to secure the parts (photo 2).

Step 5: Make the Cap Frame

1. Cut the cap front (D), cap ends (E), and cap back (F) to length. Cut 45° miters at one end of each cap end and at both ends of the cap front.

2. Join the mitered corners by drilling pilot holes through the joints (photo 3). Counterbore the holes. Fasten the pieces with glue and 2½" deck screws. Clamp the cap front and cap ends to the front of your worktable to hold them while you drive the screws.

3. Fasten the cap back between the cap ends with deck screws, making sure the back edges are flush. Set the cap frame on the planter bin so the back edges are flush. Drill pilot holes and counterbore them. Drive 2½" deck screws through the cap frame and into the side and end cleats.

Step 6: Make the Trellis

1. The trellis is made from pieces in a crosshatch pattern. The exact number and placement of the pieces is up to you—use the same spacing we used (see Drawing) or create your own.

Temporary spacers hold the posts in position while the rails are attached.

2. Cut the end posts (G), center post (H) and rails (I, J, K) to length. Lay the end posts and center post together side by side with their bottom edges flush so you can gang-mark the rail positions.

3. Use a square as a guide for drawing lines across all three posts, 18" up from the bottom. Draw the next line 7½" up from the first. Draw additional lines across the posts, spaced 7½" apart.

4. Cut two 7"-wide scrap blocks and use them to separate the posts as you assemble the trellis. Attach the rails to the posts in the sequence shown in the Diagram, using 2½" screws (photo 4). Alternate from the fronts to the backs of the posts when installing the rails.

Step 7: Apply Finishing Touches

1. Fasten the trellis to the back of the planter bin so the bottoms of the posts rest on the top edge of the base. Drill pilot holes in the posts. Counterbore the holes. Drive 2½" deck screws through the posts and into the cap frame. With a 1"-diameter spade bit, drill a pair of drainage holes in each bottom board. Stain the project with an exterior wood stain.

Planter with Hanging Trellis

TOOLS & MATERIALS

(3) 1 × 2" × 8' cedar	(1) ¾ × 4" × 4' ext. plywood	Miter saw
(3) 1 × 6" × 8' cedar	(2) ⅜ × 2-½" eyebolts	Clamps
(1) 2 × 4" × 10' cedar	Straightedge cutting guide	Compass
(2) 4 × 4" × 8' cedar	Brad nails or finish nails	Drill
(1) 2 × 2" × 6' cedar	Circular saw or table saw	Handsaw
(2) ⅜" locknuts	Tape measure	Eye and ear protection
Deck screws (2", 3")	Jigsaw	Work gloves
(4) ⅜" flat washers		

You don't need a large yard—or any yard at all for that matter—to have a garden. Planting in containers makes it possible to cultivate a garden just about anywhere. A container garden can be as simple as a small flowering annual planted in a single 4-inch pot or as elaborate as a variety of shrubs, flowering plants, and ornamental grasses planted in a large stationary planter.

This planter project combines a couple of different container options to create a larger garden in a relatively small space. The base is an 18 × 30-inch planter box that is large enough to hold several small plants, a couple of medium-sized plants, or one large plant. It features a trellis back that can be covered by climbing plants.

In addition to the planter and trellis, this project features two plant hangers that extend out from the back posts. Adding a couple of hanging plant baskets further extends the garden display without increasing the space taken up by the planter.

This project is easiest to build with a table saw, miter saw, jigsaw, and drill/driver. If you don't have access to a table saw, use a circular saw or jigsaw and straightedge to rip the 1 × 6 siding boards. An even easier option is to replace the 2¾-inch-wide siding

This efficient planter combines a box for container gardening with a climbing trellis and a pair of profiled arms for hanging potted plants.

boards with 3½-inch-wide 1 × 4s. This modification makes the planter 4½ inches taller, so you also have to make the front posts 24½ inches long instead of 20 inches long and add 4½ inches to the front posts trim.

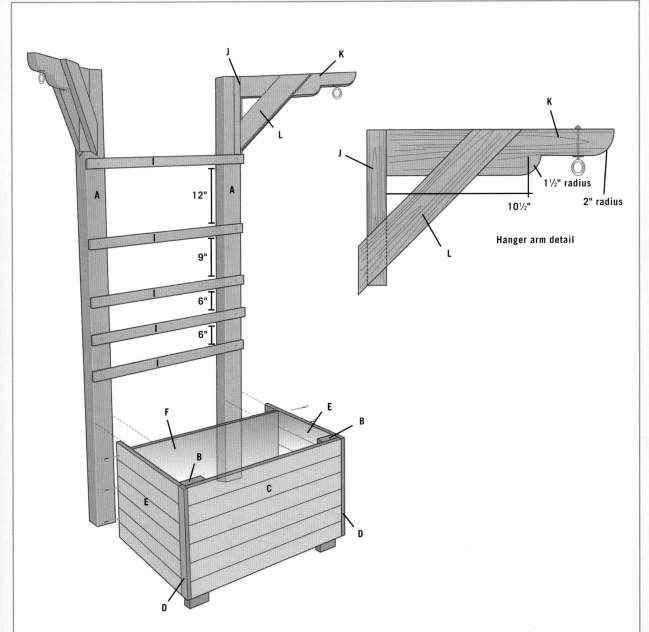

12"

9"

6"

6"

1½" radius

2" radius

10½"

Hanger arm detail

CUTTING LIST

KEY	PART	NO.	DIMENSION	MATERIAL
A	Back posts	2	3½ × 3½ × 72"	Cedar
B	Front posts	2	1½ × 3½ × 20"	Cedar
C	Front siding	6	¾ × 2¾ × 30"	Cedar
D	Front post trim	2	¾ × 1½ × 18"	Cedar
E	Side siding	12	¾ × 2¾ × 21½"	Cedar
F	Back panel	1	¾ × 18 × 30"	Ext. plywood
G	Bottom supports*	2	¾ × 1½ × 22¼"	Cedar

KEY	PART	NO.	DIMENSION	MATERIAL
H	Bottom panel*	1	¾ × 22¼ × 30"	Ext. plywood
I	Climbing rails	5	¾ × 1½ × 30"	Cedar
J	Hanger backs	2	1½ × 1½ × 12"	Cedar
K	Hanger arms	2	1½ × 3½ × 18"	Cedar
L	Hanger braces	4	1½ × 3½ × 18"	Cedar

*Not shown

How to Build a Planter with Hanging Trellis

Cut the Base Parts

Cutting the front posts (2 × 4) and back posts (4 × 4) to length is easy. Cutting the hanger parts is a bit trickier, primarily because the plant hangers splay out from the corners of the posts at a 45-degree angle. The top, outside post corners must be beveled to create flat mounting surfaces for the hangers. Mark the bevel cut lines on the outside and front faces of the posts (photo 1). Tilt the shoe of a jigsaw to 45-degree and bevel-cut along the layout lines (photo 2). Use a handsaw to make a stop cut that meets the bottom of the bevel cut in each back post, forming a shoulder (photo 3). Rip-cut some 1 × 6 stock to 2¾ inches wide (photo 4) using a table saw or a circular saw and a straightedge cutting guide. Cut six 30-inch-long pieces and twelve 21½-inch-long pieces to make the siding strips.

Also use a circular saw or table saw to cut the bottom and back panels to length and width. Cut 1½-inch-long, 3½-inch-wide notches out of the front corners of the bottom panel. Cut the front post trim, bottom supports, and back climbing rails to length from 1 × 2 boards.

Assemble the Base Planter

Attach the front siding strips to the front posts with 2-inch deck screws. Align the ends of the siding pieces flush with the sides of the front legs. Leave a ¼-inch space between the siding boards. Drive one screw through each end of each siding board and into the front legs. Drill a countersunk pilot hole for each screw. Attach the front post trim pieces to the front posts with three or four 2-inch brad nails or finish

Mark the post bevel cuts. The lines at the top of each back post should be drawn 1" out from the corner and should run down the post for 12".

Cut the bevels. Tilt the foot of a jigsaw at a 45° angle so it will ride smoothly on the post face and follow the bevel cutting line. Make a bevel cut along the layout line.

nails. Align the front edge of the trim pieces flush with the front face of the front siding. Attach the back panel to the back posts with six 2-inch screws. Drive three screws into each post.

Attach the back lattice rails to the back posts. Drive one screw through each end of each climbing rail (photo 5). Refer to the construction drawing on page 000 for lattice spacing. Place the front and back assemblies on their sides and install siding on the side that's facing up. The siding boards should be positioned against the front post trim board and flush with the back edge of the back post, spaced ¼ inch apart. Attach the siding with 2-inch screws (photo 6). Flip the project over and repeat the process to attach siding to the other side.

Attach the bottom supports to the front and back legs. The bottom of the front end of the bottom support should be flush with the bottom of the siding. The bottom of the back end of the bottom support should be positioned 2 inches up from the bottom of the back post. Drive one screw through the front end of the support and into the front leg and two screws into the back legs. Attach the bottom to the bottom supports with four 2-inch screws—two into each support.

Build the Plant Hangers

Cut the hanger backs, hanger arms, and hanger braces to length. Draw the hanger arm profile onto the side of each hanger arm, and use a compass to draw the radius profiles. Profile details are shown on the construction drawings (page 227). Use a jigsaw to cut along the profile layout lines on the hanger arms. Both ends of the hanger brace are mitered at 45 degrees, but the back or bottom end is a compound miter cut, meaning that it has both a miter and a bevel component. Cut the top-end 45-degree miters on all four braces. Then, make compound cuts at the bottom ends of the hanger braces (photo 7). Make the cuts so the beveled end faces the post when it is attached.

Make the shoulder cut. Use a handsaw to cut into the corner of the post to meet the bevel cut, creating a shoulder for the beveled corner.

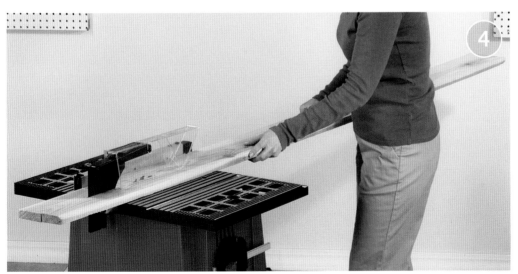

Rip 1 × 6 stock for siding. Using a table saw or a circular saw and cutting guide, rip enough material for the sides and the front to 2¾".

(continued)

Add the latticework.
Attach the horizontal climbing rails to the back posts with 2" screws. Use one screw at each lattice connection to the posts.

Install siding. Attach the siding to the front and back posts with 2" screws. After completing one side, flip the project and complete the other side. Then, install siding strips on the front.

Cut the hanger brace angles. After cutting a flat 45° miter in the top end of the hanger brace, make a compound bevel/miter cut in the bottom end so it will fit flat against the bevel cut in the post.

Drill a ⅜-inch-diameter hole through the top of each hanger arm. Locate the hole 3 inches in from the end of the hanger arm. Fasten one eyebolt, two flat washers, and a locknut through each hanger arm. Attach the hanger back to the back end of the hanger arm with two 3-inch screws. Position a 2 × 2 hanger back and a 2 × 4 hanger arm against the beveled corner of each back post. Drive two 3-inch screws through the hanger back and into the back posts. Attach the hanger braces to the hanger back and hanger arm with 2-inch screws (photo 8). Make sure the hanger arms remain perpendicular to the posts when you attach the braces.

Line the container. Attach 4-mil black plastic liner with ⅜" stainless steel staples. Overlap the plastic in the corners and leave a small gap along the back bottom edge for drainage.

Fill Planter

The planter itself is lined with heavy (at least 4-mil thick) black plastic sheeting. Cut the sheeting pieces that cover the sides, front, and bottom several inches oversized so they overlap in the corners. Cut the back sheeting the same size as the back panel. Attach the plastic to the inside faces of the planter with staples (photo 9). Start with the bottom sheet, overlap the sides on the bottom, and then overlap the front over the sides and bottom. Finally overlap the back over the sides, leaving a small gap between the bottom of the back sheet and the bottom sheet to allow water to drain out. Fill the planter with potting soil and add your plants.

TIP: Adding a few inches of gravel to the bottom of the planting compartment allows for better drainage.

Install the hanger braces. Clamp the hanger braces to the hanger arms and hanger backs. Attach the hanger braces with 2" screws driven into the hanger back and into the hanger arm. Drive two screws at each connection.

Solar Produce Dryer

A solar dryer is a drying tool that makes it possible to air-dry produce even when conditions are less than ideal. This dryer is easy to make, lightweight, and is space efficient. The dryer makes a great addition to your greenhouse.

The dryer, which is made of cedar, utilizes a salvaged window for completion. But you will have to adjust the dimensions given here for the size window that you find. The key to successful solar drying is to check the dryer frequently to make sure that it stays in the sun. If the air becomes cool and damp, the food will become a haven for bacteria. In a sunny area, your produce will dry in a couple days. Add a thermometer to the inside of your dryer box, and check on the temperature frequently—it should stay between 95 and 145 degrees Fahrenheit.

Based on the cold frame platform seen on pages 178 to 181, this solar dryer lets you dry fruit and vegetables quickly, naturally, and in a more sanitary fashion than simply air-drying.

SOLAR PRODUCE DRYER

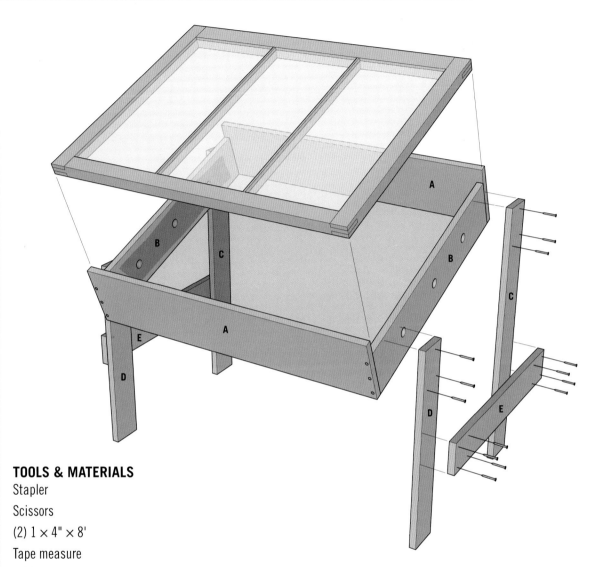

TOOLS & MATERIALS
Stapler

Scissors

(2) $1 \times 4" \times 8'$

Tape measure

Drill

Deck screws ($1\frac{1}{2}$", 2")

Brad nails

Hole saw bit

Staples

Circular saw

Screen retainer strip

Insect mesh

(1) $1 \times 8" \times 8'$

Window sash

(1) $1 \times 6" \times 8'$

Eye and ear protection

Work gloves

CUTTING LIST

KEY	PART	NO.	DIMENSION	MATERIAL
A	Front/back	2	$\frac{7}{8} \times 7\frac{1}{2} \times 34\frac{3}{4}"$	Cedar
B	Side	2	$\frac{7}{8} \times 5\frac{1}{2} \times 27\frac{1}{8}"$	Cedar
C	Leg (tall)	2	$\frac{7}{8} \times 3\frac{1}{2} \times 30"$	Cedar
D	Leg (short)	2	$\frac{7}{8} \times 3\frac{1}{2} \times 22"$	Cedar
E	Brace	2	$\frac{7}{8} \times 3\frac{1}{2} \times 24"$	Cedar

Insect mesh—fiberglass $28\frac{7}{8} \times 34\frac{3}{4}"$

How to Build a Solar Dryer

Install the mesh. Staple the screen to the frame. Then tack the retainer strips over the screen to the frame with 3 to 4 brad nails per side. Trim off the excess mesh.

Assemble the box. Attach the wider boards for the frame by driving 2" screws through the faces of the 1 × 8" boards into the ends of the 1 × 6" boards. There will be a difference in height between these pairs of boards so that the window sash can sit flush in the recess created.

Build the stand. Attach each 24" board to a 30" board (in the back) and a 22" board (in the front) with 1½" deck screws. Then attach the finished posts to the frame with three 1½" deck screws in each post.

Drill three 1" holes for ventilation in each 1 × 6" board equally spaced along the length of the board, leaving 5" of room on each end for the posts. Staple leftover insect mesh behind the ventilation holes on the inside of the frame.

Finish the project by sliding the window sash into place.

Resources

BC Greenhouse Builders
www.bcgreenhouses.com
(888) 391-4433

Black & Decker
www.blackanddecker.com

Charley's Greenhouse & Garden
www.charleysgreenhouse.com
(800) 322-4707

ePlastics
www.eplastics.com
(800) 474-3688

Grandio Greenhouses
www.grandiogreenhouses.com
(866) 448-8231

Growers Supply
www.growerssupply.com
(800) 476-9715

Growing Spaces Growing Domes
geodesic-greenhouse-kits.com
(970) 731-2120

Juliana Greenhouses
www.julianagreenhouses.com
(877) 628-9571

Outdoor Living Today
www.outdoorlivingtoday.com
(888) 658-1658

Solexx Greenhouse & Greenhouse Covering
www.solexx.com
(877) 476-5399

Studio Shed
www.studio-shed.com
(888) 900-3933

Sturdi-Built Greenhouse Manufacturing Company
www.sturdi-built.com
(800) 334-4115

Sunglo Greenhouses
www.sunglogreenhouses.com
(425) 251-8005

Photo Credits

BC Greenhouse Builders
11, 23 (bottom left), 60 (top left), 65 (bottom)

Charley's Greenhouse & Garden
8, 54, 56 (bottom), 60 (top right, bottom), 62 (bottom), 64 (top)

Clive Nichols
6

Elizabeth Whiting & Associates
18 (Michael Harris)

Dreamstime
29

ePlastics
24 (right)

Getty Images
30 (Magnus Persson), 40 (Peter Anderson)

Grandio Greenhouses
62 (top), 64 (bottom), 65 (top)

Growers Supply
46, 63 (top left)

Growing Spaces
58 (top), 63 (bottom)

Juliana America
28

North Florida Research and Education Center
43 (Robert Hochmuth)

Outdoor Living Today
57 (bottom left), 63 (top right)

Photolibrary
42 (Rick Lew)

Renaissance Conservatories
47

Solexx Greenhouses and Greenhouse Coverings
57 (top), 59 (top)

Shutterstock
20 (top right, Ivan_Sabo), 21 (bottom left, Frank L Junior), 21 (bottom right, www. sandatlas.org), 33 (Imfoto), 44 (bottom, Grandpa), 148–149 (losmandarinas), 151 (left, Stephanie Bidouze), 152 (right, donikz), 153 (top left, Michael Tatman), 168 (Sveten), 176–177 (jean morrison)

Solar Innovations
31 (left), 39 (top)

Studio Shed
55

Sturdi-Built Greenhouse Manufacturing Co.
15, 22 (bottom), 24 (left), 31 (right), 32, 41, 58 (bottom), 61

Sunglo Greenhouses
56 (top), 57 (bottom right), 59 (bottom)

Metric Conversion Charts

METRIC CONVERSIONS

TO CONVERT:	TO:	MULTIPLY BY:
Inches	Millimeters	25.4
Inches	Centimeters	25.4
Feet	Meters	0.305
Yards	Meters	0.914
Square inches	Square centimeters	6.45
Square feet	Square meters	0.093
Square yards	Square meters	0.836
Ounces	Milliliters	30.0
Pints (U.S.)	Liters	0.473 (Imp. 0.568)
Quarts (U.S.)	Liters	0.946 (Imp. 1.136)
Gallons (U.S.)	Liters	3.785 (Imp. 4.546)
Ounces	Grams	28.4
Pounds	Kilograms	0.454

TO CONVERT:	TO:	MULTIPLY BY:
Millimeters	Inches	0.039
Centimeters	Inches	0.394
Meters	Feet	3.28
Meters	Yards	1.09
Square centimeters	Square inches	0.155
Square meters	Square feet	10.8
Square meters	Square yards	1.2
Milliliters	Ounces	.033
Liters	Pints (U.S.)	2.114 (Imp. 1.76)
Liters	Quarts (U.S.)	1.057 (Imp. 0.88)
Liters	Gallons (U.S.)	0.264 (Imp. 0.22)
Grams	Ounces	0.035
Kilograms	Pounds	2.2

CONVERTING TEMPERATURES

Convert degrees Fahrenheit (F) to degrees Celsius (C) by following this simple formula: Subtract 32 from the Fahrenheit temperature reading. Then, multiply that number by 5/9. For example, 77°F - 32 = 45. 45 × 5/9 = 25°C.

To convert degrees Celsius to degrees Fahrenheit, multiply the Celsius temperature reading by 9/5. Then, add 32. For example, 25°C × 9/5 = 45. 45 + 32 = 77°F.

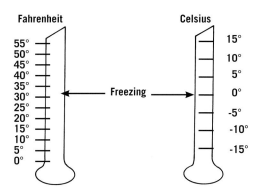

METRIC PLYWOOD PANELS

Metric plywood panels are commonly available in two sizes: 1,200 mm × 2,400 mm and 1,220 mm × 2,400 mm, which is roughly equivalent to a 4 × 8-ft. sheet. Standard and Select sheathing panels come in standard thicknesses, while Sanded grade panels are available in special thicknesses.

STANDARD SHEATHING GRADE		SANDED GRADE	
7.5 mm	(5/16 in.)	6 mm	(4/17 in.)
9.5 mm	(3/8 in.)	8 mm	(5/16 in.)
12.5 mm	(1/2 in.)	11 mm	(7/16 in.)
15.5 mm	(5/8 in.)	14 mm	(9/16 in.)
18.5 mm	(3/4 in.)	17 mm	(2/3 in.)
20.5 mm	(13/16 in.)	19 mm	(3/4 in.)
22.5 mm	(7/8 in.)	21 mm	(13/16 in.)
25.5 mm	(1 in.)	24 mm	(15/16 in.)

LUMBER DIMENSIONS

NOMINAL - U.S.	ACTUAL - U.S. (IN INCHES)	METRIC
1 × 2	3/4 × 1 1/2	19 × 38 mm
1 × 3	3/4 × 2 1/2	19 × 64 mm
1 × 4	3/4 × 3 1/2	19 × 89 mm
1 × 5	3/4 × 4 1/2	19 × 114 mm
1 × 6	3/4 × 5 1/2	19 × 140 mm
1 × 7	3/4 × 6 1/4	19 × 159 mm
1 × 8	3/4 × 7 1/4	19 × 184 mm
1 × 10	3/4 × 9 1/4	19 × 235 mm
1 × 12	3/4 × 11 1/4	19 × 286 mm
1 1/4 × 4	1 × 3 1/2	25 × 89 mm
1 1/4 × 6	1 × 5 1/2	25 × 140 mm
1 1/4 × 8	1 × 7 1/4	25 × 184 mm
1 1/4 × 10	1 × 9 1/4	25 × 235 mm
1 1/4 × 12	1 × 11 1/4	25 × 286 mm
1 1/2 × 4	1 1/4 × 3 1/2	32 × 89 mm
1 1/2 × 6	1 1/4 × 5 1/2	32 × 140 mm
1 1/2 × 8	1 1/4 × 7 1/4	32 × 184 mm
1 1/2 × 10	1 1/4 × 9 1/4	32 × 235 mm
1 1/2 × 12	1 1/4 × 11 1/4	32 × 286 mm
2 × 4	1 1/2 × 3 1/2	38 × 89 mm
2 × 6	1 1/2 × 5 1/2	38 × 140 mm
2 × 8	1 1/2 × 7 1/4	38 × 184 mm
2 × 10	1 1/2 × 9 1/4	38 × 235 mm
2 × 12	1 1/2 × 11 1/4	38 × 286 mm
3 × 6	2 1/2 × 5 1/2	64 × 140 mm
4 × 4	3 1/2 × 3 1/2	89 × 89 mm
4 × 6	3 1/2 × 5 1/2	89 × 140 mm

LIQUID MEASUREMENT EQUIVALENTS

1 Pint	= 16 Fluid Ounces	= 2 Cups
1 Quart	= 32 Fluid Ounces	= 2 Pints
1 Gallon	= 128 Fluid Ounces	= 4 Quarts

DRILL BIT GUIDE

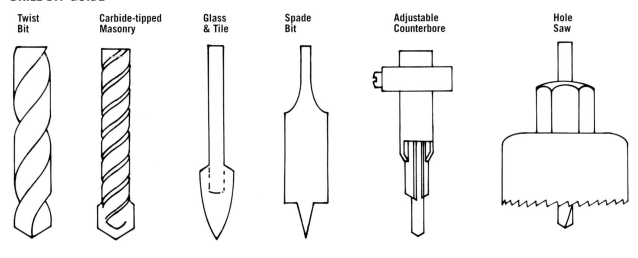

Twist Bit   Carbide-tipped Masonry   Glass & Tile   Spade Bit   Adjustable Counterbore   Hole Saw

NAILS

Nail lengths are identified by numbers from 4 to 60 followed by the letter "d," which stands for "penny." For general framing and repair work, use common or box nails. Common nails are best suited to framing work where strength is important. Box nails are smaller in diameter than common nails, which makes them easier to drive and less likely to split wood. Use box nails for light work and thin materials. Most common and box nails have a cement or vinyl coating that improves their holding power.

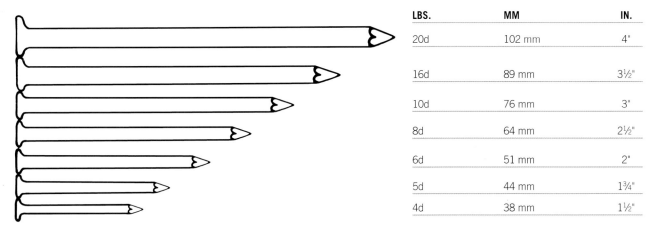

LBS.	MM	IN.
20d	102 mm	4"
16d	89 mm	3½"
10d	76 mm	3"
8d	64 mm	2½"
6d	51 mm	2"
5d	44 mm	1¾"
4d	38 mm	1½"

COUNTERBORE, SHANK & PILOT HOLE DIAMETERS

SCREW SIZE	COUNTERBORE DIAMETER FOR SCREW HEAD (IN INCHES)	CLEARANCE HOLE FOR SCREW SHANK (IN INCHES)	PILOT HOLE DIAMETER	
			HARD WOOD (IN INCHES)	SOFT WOOD (IN INCHES)
#1	.146 (⁹⁄₆₄)	⁵⁄₆₄	³⁄₆₄	¹⁄₃₂
#2	¼	³⁄₃₂	³⁄₆₄	¹⁄₃₂
#3	¼	⁷⁄₆₄	¹⁄₁₆	³⁄₆₄
#4	¼	⅛	¹⁄₁₆	³⁄₆₄
#5	¼	⅛	⁵⁄₆₄	¹⁄₁₆
#6	⁵⁄₁₆	⁹⁄₆₄	³⁄₃₂	⁵⁄₆₄
#7	⁵⁄₁₆	⁵⁄₃₂	³⁄₃₂	⁵⁄₆₄
#8	⅜	¹¹⁄₆₄	⅛	³⁄₃₂
#9	⅜	¹¹⁄₆₄	⅛	³⁄₃₂
#10	⅜	³⁄₁₆	⅛	⁷⁄₆₄
#11	½	³⁄₁₆	⁵⁄₃₂	⁹⁄₆₄
#12	½	⁷⁄₃₂	⁹⁄₆₄	⅛

Index